To Weezie,
the best saxophone player in the world.

To Curtis (who got it), Paul (age 11), Amber, who put her dad in jail (no baby, your daddy put himself in jail), to Derek whose family is "just feedin' out beef cattle since there ain't no money left in dairy." To the boy in Portsmouth who asked, "Is it okay to write a poem about how racist a person is?" (Yes, please do. We need to talk about it.) To Hector in the hooded sweatshirt, to the brawny boys who had a lift-a-thon to sponsor my visit because they love poetry, to the boy in Kokomo whose girlfriend committed suicide (I hope you found a forum for her poems), and to Jamal and Janeka (hope it works out). To Jessica, whose mom is never home to sign her stuff, to the girl with the corn rows in Van Wert who asked me if I know Britney Spears, and to Whitney, who took time to write to me this year to tell me she thinks I have potential. And to the thousands of kids whose poetry books I've signed who know that turbulent waters also run deep. Keep writing.

Practical Poetry

A Nonstandard Approach to Meeting Content-Area Standards

Sara Holbrook

HEINEMANN
PORTSMOUTH, NH

Heinemann

A division of Reed Elsevier Inc.

361 Hanover Street

Portsmouth, NH 03801–3912

www.heinemann.com

Offices and agents throughout the world

The author and publisher wish to thank those who have generously given permission to reprint borrowed material:

"911" by Michael Salinger from *Neon*. Copyright © 2002 by Michael Salinger. Published by Bottom Dog Press, Bowling Green State University. Reprinted by permission of the author.

"Adrenaline" from *By Definition* by Sara Holbrook. Copyright © 2003 by Sara Holbrook. Published by Boyds Mills Press. Reprinted by permission.

Credits continue on page 173.

Library of Congress Cataloging-in-Publication Data

Holbrook, Sara.

Practical poetry : a nonstandard approach to meeting content-area
     standards / Sara Holbrook.
          p.   cm.
     ISBN 0-325-00767-5 (alk. paper)
     1.   Poetry—Study and teaching (Middle school)—United States.
     2.   Language arts (Middle school)—United States.   I.   Title.
LB1575.H64 2005
372.64—dc22   2004020530

Consulting editor: Harvey Daniels
Editor: Leigh Peake
Production: Elizabeth Valway
Cover design: Catherine Hawkes, Cat and Mouse
Cover photo: Debbra Bohne
Interior design: Jenny Jensen Greenleaf
Chapter opener photos: Sara Holbrook and Katie Lufkin
Composition: Publishers' Design and Production Services, Inc.
Manufacturing: Steve Bernier

Printed in the United States of America on acid-free paper
09 08 07 06 05   RRD   1 2 3 4 5

Contents

Foreword

I can still remember the first time I heard Sara Holbrook perform her poem, "Naked." It was at the end of a long day of professional development, yet the audience made no move to leave as she began, "I remember the first time I. . . ." When her poem ended, we sat in silence for several seconds—stunned with the enormity of our experience of World War II through a poem. What we knew of war had been transformed because Sara had been able to capture one moment of war's inhumanity, wrap that moment in her experience, and give it to us in words that would forever impact our perceptions of war. As I wiped away tears, I couldn't help but wish all children could experience their study of history in such a powerful way. With the publication of *Practical Poetry*, all children can.

Practical Poetry is both a collection of solid instructional strategies and a reminder that the strategies are only significant if students want to read and write on the other side of our instruction. This is a book that shows us how to make poetry a natural part of content reading and writing. Each of the strategies has student samples where young readers and writers demonstrate their knowledge of content and writing. At a time when we struggle to make every moment of our teaching days count, Sara gives us many strategies for exploding that moment through poetry. There are chapters devoted to each of the core content areas and each of those has poetry exercises that can help students think and write about their content knowledge. The exercises are solidly embedded in significant content and correlated to national content standards. Sara says this functional poetry is ". . . like functional pottery. This is poetry that holds water."

If the book only provided effective strategies, it would be a fine contribution to the field. But, this book goes well beyond that. For those of us who have had the good fortune of hearing Sara perform her poetry, we can hear her voice in every word of *Practical Poetry*. Her humor, her love of children, and her love of the right word are over and under all of the teaching in this book. In Sara's Introduction, she tells us that poetry "serves as a bridge to understanding" and I agree. Sara's poetry helps us bridge our beliefs about what is best for children while still addressing the mandates that can occur in a standards-based curriculum. This book is a gift for our teaching heads and our teaching hearts.

In *Teaching with Fire: Poetry That Sustains the Courage to Teach*, Sam Intrator and Megan Scribner remind us of the power of poetry: "Poetry has a way of slipping past ego and intellect to speak directly to the heart about matters of great moment. And when the heart has received a message, we find it hard to turn away, even if the message engages us with issues that yield to no easy fix; if that were not the case, why would so many people still be working toward a world of truth, justice, and mercy?" Sara Holbrook's *Practical Poetry* does just that. She has given us passageways into those classroom "matters of great moment" and writing paths to record what we saw while there.

Sara says that anytime we can say, "I saw what I saw and it looked like this," we have a poem. *Practical Poetry* is Sara's poem for educators. She saw what she saw—something was missing in our students' writing lives. But, she didn't stop there. She saw what she saw and then did something about it. She gave us a bridge—to content, to standards, to the lives of our students, and to the poet in each of us.

Janet Allen

Acknowledgments

No book is ever the product of the work of one person. I have had discerning advice, inspiration, and encouragement from a community of friends and family who give new meaning to the term "support group."

First, thank you to my daughters Katie Lufkin and Kelly Weist, who are a continuing source of inspiration and support. Thank you, Katie, for allowing me into your classroom and teaming with me to unearth the student samples in this book. Thank you, Kelly, for managing the business of my writing career, without which I never would have had time to write this book. It is because of you both that I became the poet formerly known as Mom. You have taught me everything I know about love.

A huge thank-you to Smokey (Harvey) Daniels for saying, "Looks like a book to me," and then making sure it became one. You have a unique blend of foresight, patience, and wisdom and positivity that is so needed in this world. That coupled with a passion for educational excellence and the tenacity of a pit bull make you a bonzer ally.

Serial thank-you's to my second family, Michael Salinger and sons Maxwel and Frank, who ping-ponged ideas around with me throughout the process and didn't complain too much about the metaphorical and real stacked-up dishes while I holed up in my office. Special thanks to Michael for sharing some of his own writing within.

Thank you to a whole lot of teachers who took the chance on inviting a poet to their schools, thereby helping to keep me and an entire genre of literature alive when so many forces from television to computer games seem to be engaged in contrary conspiracies. Special thanks to Kris Watkins for inspiring the format of this book. Thanks to Dr. Nancy McCracken for believing in me early on and for introducing me to Dr. Lynne Alvine, who introduced me to Smokey. Thanks to Anne Cobb, Dr. Jill Perry, LeeAnn Spillane, Christine Landaker Charbeneau, and Dr. Janet Allen for helping a poet understand pedagogy. Thanks to Debbie and the Fitness Fanatics for helping me get the kinks out after hours hunched over the keyboard.

Thanks to Kent Brown for generously allowing reprints of many poems originally published by Boyds Mills Press. Thank you to the students who have contributed work to this manuscript, particularly the writers at Bay Village Middle School (Ohio) and Gompers Secondary School (San Diego, CA).

Finally, thanks to the creative and professional staff at Heinemann, including Alan Huisman for his brilliant editorial surgery, Elizabeth Valway, and Leigh Peake for not giving up on me.

Introduction

What architect decided schools should have a separate art room down the hall? What a baffling blunder. Suddenly all art forms are perceived as "specials," separate from the real work of education. A time for serious teachers to plan their lessons. An indulgence for kids who are already overindulged, or a nuisance for those scrambling to catch up. Poetry is relegated to an isolated two-week unit in May—if all other requirements have been fulfilled.

But, curriculum standards! Assessments! Tests and more tests! What about state and national standards? (Can world and intergalactic standards be far behind?) Teachers are pressured to see that all students achieve common goals. There are so many facts to digest at this point that we can't afford just to sit around and make stuff up. It's only logical to close the door on that art room once and for all.

Or is it?

Art is not dissimilar from history, mathematics, and science any more than poetry is dissimilar from other forms of writing. Every subject taught in school, when brought to its highest level, becomes an art form, be it geometry, biology, auto mechanics, or the study of language. The jumping-off place is that moment when the knowledge gained in our field of expertise carries us into the uncharted water of new ideas and we manage to stay afloat, buoyed by what we've already learned. It's true of the poet, the heart surgeon, the cellist, and that guy at Superlube who welds some metal together to make a part for eighty bucks that costs ten times as much from the dealer.

Creativity isn't just making stuff up. It is using familiar tools to make something that wasn't there before. It is a stew made up of three main ingredients—knowledge, confidence, and leisure time. And though you may get a different response from a ballerina or a mathematician, it is my job as a poet to say that we can offer these ingredients to students through the study of poetry in all content areas.

By integrating poetry into classrooms, we can learn about history firsthand from the people who were there. We can use words to define mathematical equations and scientific conclusions. What good is a scientific discovery if it can't be put into words and published? By studying poetry, we learn another language for love besides the expletives we hear on the street. We encounter emotions like anger, sadness, or loneliness expressed in ways we can understand. This goes well beyond the state standards and. . . .

Hold it!

You can't get beyond the standards until they are met, can you? You can't afford to waste time on otherworldly froufrou poetry in the middle of a geometry lesson when the bottom line is banging on your classroom door demanding totals and percentages. Right?

Give me a few more paragraphs, and let's see if I can make poetry and standards keep much closer company.

First, let's go to Kris Watkins' seventh-grade classroom in Betsy Layne, Kentucky. (This trek may be a little off the beaten path, but stick with me—Betsy Layne is a real place.) Last fall, I was teaching a writing workshop there. After the first class, Kris walked over to a laminated, multicolored, poster-board chart of numbered goals on a wall and pointed out how my lesson fit in.

"Wow," I said with august poetic articulation, "cool." I was already feeling proud for having found Betsy Layne all by myself, and my mind was spinning after a forty-five-minute writing lesson that had us all panting at the bell. As an afterthought, as I reached for my water bottle, I asked, "So what's this list all about?"

Kris patiently pointed out the boldface heading. These were the "Kentucky State Standards," and she had them posted on the wall. Clearly, Kris was not directing the grim death march to the annual test I had witnessed in some other schools. Her classroom was alive with enthusiastic students, jumping with questions and eager to try out new approaches to writing. Kris explained what had prompted her to post the standards in her class: "It was a combination of a guideline from my principal, Mrs. Calhoun, who wanted us to have our program of studies for the State of Kentucky visible and handy at all times and a need to offer a visual aid to my students. I want my students to be able to connect our objectives for the day to a visual image. I emphasize how these objectives connect to our core content and program of studies and direct their attention to the colored cards as I explain the exact standard being dealt with in that unit or lesson."

"Oh," I replied (sometimes I'm just over-the-top with this poetic eloquence thing). "And poetry fits in there?" I gaped at the numbered list. So many items.

Kris explained some more. "Poetry opens a world of sensory experiences in any content area and should be used to reinforce every subject taught, so connecting standards to poetry just makes it easier for everyone to use that form of writing."

"*Oh!*" Now that *was* cool. Encouraging kids to write poetry based on standards issued from the state. Very cool, indeed.

And the impetus for this book. I went back to my poetry writing workshops and looked at them with a different eye. Could the writing of poetry be incorporated into classrooms not in addition to meeting the standards, but for the very purpose of meeting them?

To study poetry is to study language, powerful language. Poetry is both concise and precise, two of the most important elements of effective communication. Anytime we say, "I saw what I saw and it looked like this," that is a poem, as well as an essential tool in all academic disciplines.

I worked in public relations for many years, both as a writer of press releases, brochures, reports, and speeches and as a supervisor of other such writers. On the side, I was writing my poetry. A hobby, of course. But the most amazing thing started to happen. The more sand-kicking, arms-crossed, boo-boo-lip poems I wrote, the better my speeches became, the better my press releases became, and the more promotions I received. In reflection more than a decade later, I can attribute my business success directly to—of all things—poetry. Why? Because the language of business is extremely precise, as the warranty disclaimer for any product will attest. When this requirement for precision is coupled with the limitations of column inches or thirty-second sound bites, knowledge of the poet's distilled language is a definite asset.

Of course poets also go looking for the truth, which may or may not be a useful skill in public relations, but that's another issue.

I believe in functional poetry. Much like functional pottery, this is poetry that holds water. It makes sense to keep it around. It does something for us. Makes a connection. It doesn't just sit there on the shelf and look mysterious. Art for art's sake is a silly philosophy that relegates us to that room down the hall in which we run the risk of losing our connection to the real world. I would argue that art is for the sake of everyone. Art, poetry included, should be an intramural event, not simply a spectator sport.

The poet uses words as a means to an end, but that end is not simply the poem. The end is the impact the poem has on the writer and his audience, her audience. That audience may be a single friend, a classroom, a nation, or just the poet. We write poetry to make our individual ideas heard, and these ideas must not be limited to language arts class, another silly idea. When we succeed, when we create a poem that serves as a bridge toward understanding, that is communication—an indispensable standard of learning.

Practical Poetry

Practical Poetry

A Rationale

Let's get serious. It's a new century, and a practical, demanding world waits outside that school yard. Is poetry more than a luxury, a taste of sweet not to be overindulged? Does it have a life outside language arts class? Does it belong in the curriculum at all in the age of Star Wars and CNN?

Naturally, my answer to such questions is a resounding yes. I am, after all, a poet and prejudiced in favor of the genre. However, I also know many teachers who agree with me. How do we convince those who write the school curriculum that poetry is not just the icing on the learning cake, but in fact is among the essential ingredients needed to make the cake rise?

This book is meant to help teachers meet standards in four major content areas—mathematics, language arts, science, and social studies—by linking poetry writing exercises to many of them. The idea is that poetry is one more instrument in a teacher's arsenal for reinforcing learning in all subjects.

What this book does not presume to do is show teachers how to meet all the standards in all the content areas all the time. It is also not about testing, although at the end of every exercise I suggest how one could assess students' work. Like it or not, grades have meaning to parents and kids. My feeling is that assessment should encourage students to write more, not silence

1

them. Beyond that student poetry itself is a way of assessing content-area learning.

After immersing myself in these standards for a few months, I'm convinced they have gotten a bad rap by being lumped with the current testing craze. Standards have not been designed by a corporation to sell a curriculum or program, as many standardized tests are. Nor is anyone running for office based on their outcomes. The only people meant to profit from content standards are teachers and kids. In fact, the standards themselves are thoughtful, logical, and comprehensive, leading students to acquire skills that should indeed help them with their schoolwork and life skills.

Standardized tests that compare twelve-year-olds in rural Alabama, Anchorage, New York City, and everywhere in between have never made much sense to me, but they are a reality. What I know about realities is that, like potholes, we have to deal with them. But we needn't confine ourselves to learning what's on tests, which is very limiting, nor should we abandon all the standards established by folks knowledgeable in various fields.

I could never write a book that supports some of the wretched, corporate-designed, and packaged excuses for learning being undertaken in the name of raising test scores. Somebody's "scoring" big on such programs, but it isn't the kids and it isn't the teachers. Nor could I write a book to support scripted programs that limit individual initiative to asking for the bathroom pass. Those programs have very little to do with content standards or students working toward being able to live a successful life.

In my travels working as a visiting poet in schools for the past twelve years, I have seen firsthand how trapped many teachers are by the sometimes conflicting goals being set for them at all levels. What I hope is that even in areas like science and social studies, in which teaching is virtually subject to a restraining order in favor of preparing students for high-stakes language arts and math tests, writing poetry can be a tool to help teachers meet the goals.

During the past dozen years, I have seen kids write some amazing poems. I wish I could share them all with you; unfortunately, that isn't the way copyright laws work. Since I don't have a classroom of my own, I've had to rely on the teachers and librarians who relentlessly tracked down students and parents for permission to use students' work. And since middle-grade kids are as likely to be having babies as playing with dolls, I have attempted to show what students of various ages and abilities have done with the same exercise. When possible, I have also provided alternative models suited to various skill levels.

Do you stalwartly believe that creative writing in general and poetry in particular have no place in the real world? Meet my son-in-law Brian. I've known Brian since he was in high school and the center for the Bay Village Rockets football team. As a young man, he was honest, careful, and strong, but writing and poetry were never what you might call an important part of his life. (I do give him credit for listening patiently over the years to his mother-in-law's efforts.)

After two years of college, extensive special training, and a series of promotions, he is now a member of the Secret Service Emergency Response Team stationed at the White House. Basically, he dresses in all black and stands on top of the building (or elsewhere in its environs) with a machine gun. Not a job that anyone, least of all Brian, his teachers, his parents, his friends, or me, would associate with requiring writing skills. So wasn't I surprised last summer when Brian told me, "If there's one class I wish I had paid more attention to in high school, it's writing."

See, every time some joker tries to jump the fence at the White House, which apparently happens with some regularity, the agents who intercept him (not so much her) have to write a report. The report has to be precise and concise. It has to be able to stand up to lawyer scrutiny when the case finally comes to court (sometimes two years later). The writer has to say, "I saw what I saw and it looked like this," capturing an image in words. This requires keen observational skills, excellent organizational skills, and the ability to use language precisely.

I can't tell you how many times I've heard students remark, about their not-the-most-studious selves, "Hey, it's not like we're ever going to become writers." (And, worse, many administrators say it about them too.) Well, excuse me? Many successful adults were not part of the intellectual crowd as kids. We never know what our students will end up doing, but more jobs require precise writing skills than many of us think.

If your students or your administrators won't take a poet's word for this, maybe they'll believe Brian.

I have spent a great deal of time during the last few years refining the exercises in one particular teacher's classroom. In the space of three years, Katie Lufkin has taught fifth grade at Orchard Elementary School in Cleveland, Ohio, and sixth-grade science, social studies, and language arts at Bay Village Middle School in Bay Village, Ohio. She has opened her class to me on too many occasions to count, writing along with her students, offering suggestions on how to fine-tune the exercises, cluing me in on how the curriculum at her school is formulated based on standards, and persistently collecting permissions to use student work. She describes herself as "not an overhead, note-giving teacher. I am always trying to find ways to help my kids 'get it' without just giving it to them. This is my biggest challenge as a teacher." She assures me that writing poetry in her classrooms has helped her kids "get" and retain content lessons. Being able to work together to support each other's goals is very important to both of us. (You should also know that Katie is my daughter.)

Exactly how can poetry help kids "get it"? Here are some reflections, personal and professional, on how poetry can be a practical route to learning.

Writing Poetry Jogs the Memory. For me, sitting down to write is like stringing a popcorn necklace. I have to hunt around my memory for the pieces, taking extravagant care to arrange in a certain order, then I remember something else and have to unstring. Working my memory over, I prioritize, make order out of chaos, rediscover details, and put events in sequence. Poetry is a practical route to learning and remembering.

Writing Poetry Demands Keen Observation. Most students suffer from some kind of "decibel damage," whether from horror movie soundtracks, video game bells and whistles, boomboxes, or the evening news. Assaulted by so many stimuli at such volume, they have become highly skilled at turning off and tuning out. A survival mechanism of the modern age, this is also a detriment to human and environmental consciousness. Writing poetry forces us to relearn the preschool adage "stop, look, and listen," to take in details that are essential to future scientists, historians, lawyers, moms, convenience store employees, and community members. We want students to do more than watch—we want them to see. Poetry is an eye opener.

Writing Poetry Requires Precise Language. Whether it's because we've become so used to listening to and speaking in media sound bites or are simply inundated with too much information, our language is becoming less concrete. We need words not only to articulate feelings and observations, but also to think clearly. Kids are way too inclined to talk in generalities: "you're bad," "that's awesome," "this sucks." Yeah, but *why* does it suck? Because it smells like that washcloth you left balled up beside the tub? Because it has less energy than a dead battery? Because, because, because . . . Poetry eschews the ready-made phrases that make up much of the dialogue kids watch on TV or learn to pass off as conversation. It enriches our vocabulary as we reach for the dictionary to find just the right word. *I saw what I saw and it looked like this.* Poetry asks the important questions and forces us to define ourselves in concrete visual terms.

Writing and Performing Poetry Stimulates Good Communication Skills. What good is knowing something if we can't communicate our ideas to others? If the best I can say for myself is a mumbled "What I did was great" while looking at my toes and kicking the dirt, no one will ever award me a grant for further study, hire me for the job of my dreams, or listen to my recommendations. Today we are inundated with mass communication, mass media, mass emails—the masses blaring and blasting at one another. Poetry remains the voice of the individual. It is naturally journalistic, expository, and persuasive. Because a poem reflects the writer's *personal* feelings or observations, that writer works carefully to craft the phrases and images necessary to do the job. This fact alone can change the tedious panning for just the right word into a gold rush. Writing poetry is like making funny faces at ourselves in the mirror; we've all tried it, but don't often talk about it. What a pity, because talking about it is what communication is all about. Encouraging students to share poems with one another—during poetry readings, at coffeehouses, on webpages, and in literary journals—spurs them to refine their writing. They will work harder at making themselves understood if they have an audience. Poetry encourages writers to be precise and concise—two of the most important components of good communication.

Writing Poetry Encourages Good Organizational Skills. The writing process is one of observing, brainstorming, sorting, and prioritizing. We observe a universe of concepts, perceptions, and sentiments and then narrow them down to precise examples that prove the point we want to make. We form patterns and images out of chaos, thereby honing our ability to organize thoughts—take a jumble of ideas and impose order. Whenever something doesn't make sense to me, I reach for a pencil and paper to try to make order out of whatever confusion is swirling between my ears. Never having been a very organized person (understatement alert), poetry is my lifeline.

Writing Poetry Encourages Reading Fluency. Poems are like potato chips; one munch is never enough. Poems beg to be reread. Whether it's light verse from Ogden Nash or a serious rap testament of Tupac's, typically we whip through a first reading, blink or giggle or gulp, and read it again. And if we like the poem a lot, we share it with a friend. Poems want to be read again and again.

Faces

Faces mirror
faces.
Looking through
our differences
can we comprehend
a community of learning
to read
past only faces
to the human heart
    within?
Can the rhythm
of our language,
its twang
and brogue
and jive,
work to keep
the solo voice,
the chorus,
and
the symphony
alive?

—SARA HOLBROOK,
Walking on the Boundaries
of Change

Writing Poetry Helps Us Learn About Ourselves and Our World. Reading is trickle-down learning; writing is building our own learning curve. Studying about the migration of the pioneers, the realities of slavery, the violence in our society, or the war in Iraq (Rowanda, Bosnia, Korea) means mastering some facts long enough to be tested on them. Writing a poem using the factual knowledge gained in history, science, math, or current events lessons places students in the action. Likewise, writing poetry about inner wars and joys helps us determine what we like, what is true, and what makes us uncomfortable. All of these lessons enhance our growth as people and community members. Poetry helps bring the world into focus, helps us understand, express, and seek a solution—invaluable lessons for students of any age.

Poetry—Written, Spoken, or Read—Is Powerful Language. Poetry has been a jungle gym in my life, a place to stretch and flip, climb to the top for a look-see, and occasionally fall and skin my nose. Poetry is so interwoven with my life that it is difficult to separate my experiences from my writing. And that's the gist of what I have to share with you, really—how I went about stringing necklaces, making faces at myself in the mirror, and swinging from monkey bars to find myself and my poetic voice.

My earnest hope is that the exercises in this book, modeled on my own learning and teaching, will help you and your students find your own respective voices. And that thus finding your own way into writing, you won't need me anymore except as an audience. Blow me away. I can't wait.

2 ~ *Language Arts*

"With all this emphasis on proficiencies, my poetry books just languish on the shelves. It's such a crime, because there is a lot of really good stuff back there." So lamented Kim Geletka, media specialist at Hilliard Elementary School, in Westlake, Ohio, on the phone recently. And then in hushed tones she confessed that when she goes to book fairs she can't resist buying more poetry even though "teachers just don't have room for poetry in their classes these days."

How do we make room for poetry in a crowded language arts curriculum? With reading proficiency tests driving the curriculum, should we?

See, poetry is like candy. Kids gobble it down. They gaggle together, giggle over it, and grind their teeth trying to create their own. Kids love poetry.

But kids like cartoons too, and we don't tune into the Cartoon Network for ideas on how to meet the standards for English and language arts. Still, as we search for ways to provide students with the "opportunities and resources to develop the language skills they need to pursue life's goals and to participate fully as informed, productive members of society" (that's a mouthful, or a planning book full as the case may be), it does make sense to look for vehicles capable of helping us attain our goals. For this reason alone, poetry needs to be taken off the shelf and reevaluated. Kids *like* it, like the way the vehicle roars and shines and toots, making them more eager to climb on board for a journey to better language skills.

And they do in the early grades. Primary teachers use poetry to teach sounds and improve reading fluency. The kids memorize bug poems and holiday chants with hand motions. They recite verse while stomping across the floors of America's classrooms. It's a virtual stampede. When I visit elementary schools, the kids are wild for poetry. They start to laugh before I pick up the microphone. They think I'm a stand-up comic.

However, by the time these same kids are in the intermediate grades and middle school, they aren't too sure about poetry any more. They are skeptical. A little confused. Poetry seems to have switched gears on them—and their teachers. It's a big leap from Shel Silverstein to Walt Whitman.

And by high school? Three kids, dressed all in black, in the back of the room, and these are our poetry fans. We have lost the rest.

What went wrong?

Somewhere in the intermediate and middle grades we lose many poetry fans because we drop the writing component from poetry units and just study poetry. We abandon the sounds of poetry, the performances and aural pleasures, and just look for meaning, which is like studying the musical score of *The Sound of Music* on the page without strings, kettledrums, and Julie Andrews. Dull.

Poetry lessons should foster a love of the genre while helping writers find their voice. Too often we ask kids to make booklets of poetry patterns and ignore the substance of the writing. This is a little like assembling a book of pictures of all the different kinds of bicycles that exist with the hope that it will teach kids how to ride. We learn to ride by riding, and we learn to write by writing.

Former Poet Laureate Billy Collins, in a lecture I heard him give in 2003 at John Carroll University, said he had once over-heard a college student utter a perfect haiku:

> When he found out, he
> Was like, Oh my God, and I
> Was like, Oh my God.

Don't you love it? Perfect pattern, you'd have to give the student an A for that: five-seven-five. The kid's got the pattern, but nothing to say.

This is a hazard when writing poetry for which the end goal is the pattern itself, not a pattern chosen to support a topic. A pattern is just the box we use to convey an idea. Complex patterns like sonnets are an acquired taste, like coffee without the taste killers. If we stack too many boxes in the poetry storage room, all the writers are going to do is trip over them.

By high school, students are studying Poetry with a capital P, and most are quite happy to leave poetry writing to the professionals. Which is not to say that many of them aren't still writing poetry. But we've instilled in these young poets a self-conscious twitch that makes them fret that what they are writing is not "good" poetry. They go underground. Instead of a classroom language experience, poetry becomes an embarrassing indulgence (like making those funny faces in the mirror). And suddenly all those rumors about poetry's being superfluous become a self-fulfilling prophecy. Poetry was not born out of the mainstream, we have kicked it to the curb.

As if poetry could be any more useless in the real world than the 5PT—the five-paragraph theme. I have lived and worked as a writer for many years. When my mother died, I did not feel compelled to write a 5PT. Nor did I after seeing *Swan Lake* or watching images of the war in Iraq. Never in my career as a business writer was I required to write a five-paragraph theme. A 5PT won't stand up in court, describe your vacation to the neighbors in mouth-watering detail, or get you a job—except as an English teacher required to spend inordinate amounts of time teaching the structure of the 5PT.

As a writer I have, however, been required to use a precise and diverse vocabulary, organize my thoughts, create images with words, construct strong leads, and speak in a voice appropriate to my audience. I need to understand point of view and metaphor and write with an economy of words. I have been called on to generate ideas through discussions with my peers; to use action

When my older daughter started kindergarten, I went to the school for some indoctrination on start times, drop-off points, paint shirts, and head lice. It was a lot to absorb. I came home in tears. Not because of the head lice alert, that was only vaguely unsettling (not *my* kid, oh how we live and learn). No, what got me worked up was the stencil discussion. The teacher pulled out a folder of holiday stencils (pumpkins, snowmen, and hearts) to explain her approach to art. She went on to explain the importance of parental involvement in the artistic development of our children—we were to post each project on the refrigerator, a new one every month.

"Don't the kids get to make their own valentine hearts?" I asked.

She laughed. Silly mom. Must be her oldest starting school.

"If I let the children make their own valentines, their hearts turn out looking like butterflies." She went on with her prepared speech without missing a beat. She was a kindergarten teacher, a woman accustomed to senseless interruptions, someone with a well-developed talent for carrying on both sides of the conversation.

My hand went back up in the air. "Excuse me."

Her smile twitched slightly as she cocked her head in my direction. "Yes?"

"What's wrong with hearts that look like butterflies?"

She laughed heartily at that one. "If their hearts don't all look the same, some of them will cry."

I'm not sure what else she talked about in that hour (clearly, I missed some key points on head lice). My mind instantly became a flutter of dying butterflies. Butterflies dead on the windshield of kindergarten. Under the tires of elementary school. Piled like cordwood beside the road to maturity. Dead butterflies everywhere. Her approach to creativity may have saved a child or two from crying, but it sent one parent home sobbing.

I remember this efficient woman every time I am invited to look at a book or a display of stencil poems, acrostics, and their many variations. Poetry is not refrigerator art, little hearts created on red (not orange or purple) construction paper pulled from the same ream, outlined by the same stencils (read formulas), pierced in exactly the same spots with pipe cleaner arrows. The format is just the box we use to carry our ideas to the world.

verbs, colorful modifiers, and sensory details; and to proofread and edit my work. I have to understand sequencing and be able to compare and contrast, incorporate dialogue, recognize voice, and be persuasive. And yes, all these writing elements can be taught through the 5PT.

But. (This is a big *but*; it deserves its own paragraph.)

But these writing elements need not be taught *exclusively* through that vehicle. There are a myriad of writing patterns we can use to teach these elements, and poetry is one.

Poetry is a series of snapshots. If we become very focused in our snapshots, we are going to be able to string them together to create vivid stories, letters, and reports. I contend that practicing writing skills through poetry will even help students produce better 5PTs for their proficiency tests.

But first, as teachers, we have to transcend the prejudices and fears of poetry instilled in us *by our* teachers. We need to view poetry as not only an end in itself, a piece of art, but as a means to an end.

The national standards for English language arts are comprehensive and interwoven. Unlike the standards in other content areas, they do not prescribe particular curriculum goals by age or grade level. Such direction is provided at state and local levels. Naturally state and local standards vary, but key terms, such as *audience, point of view, revision, inference, compare/contrast,* and so on, link them with the national standards. *Standards for the English Language Arts,* a joint publication of the International Reading Association and the National Council of Teachers of English, further defines standards. Many of the exercises in this chapter address more than one standard, as a whole or in part.

Because the national standards for English and language arts are written so broadly, often with many goals in each strand, I list them next for your reference. Each exercise in this chapter lists the specific goals, highlighted in a marginal box, that it will help students achieve. Beyond that, exercises in the math, social studies, and science chapters can also help students meet the English language arts standards.

1. Students read a wide range of print and nonprint texts to build an understanding of texts, of themselves, and of the cultures of the United States and the world; to acquire new information; to respond to the needs and demands of society and the workplace; and for personal fulfillment. Among these texts are fiction and nonfiction, classic and contemporary works.

2. Students read a wide range of literature from many periods in many genres to build an understanding of the many dimensions (e.g., philosophical, ethical, aesthetic) of human experience.

3. Students apply a wide range of strategies to comprehend, interpret, evaluate, and appreciate texts. They draw on their prior experience, their interactions with other readers and writers, their knowledge of word meaning and of other texts, their word identification strategies, and their understanding of textual features (e.g., sound–letter correspondence, sentence structure, context, graphics).

4. Students adjust their use of spoken, written, and visual language (e.g., conventions, style, vocabulary) to communicate effectively with a variety of audiences and for different purposes.

5. Students employ a wide range of strategies as they write and use different writing process elements appropriately to communicate with different audiences for a variety of purposes.

6. Students apply knowledge of language structure; language conventions (e.g., spelling and punctuation); media techniques; figurative language; and genre to create, critique, and discuss print and nonprint texts.

7. Students conduct research on issues and interests by generating ideas and questions and by posing problems. They gather, evaluate, and synthesize data from a variety of sources (e.g., print and nonprint texts, artifacts, people) to communicate their discoveries in ways that suit their purpose and audience.

8. Students use a variety of technological and information resources (e.g., libraries, databases, computer networks, videos) to gather and synthesize information and to create and communicate knowledge.

9. Students develop an understanding of and respect for diversity in language use, patterns, and dialects across cultures, ethnic groups, geographic regions, and social roles.

10. Students whose first language is not English make use of their first language to develop competency in the English

language arts and to develop an understanding of content across the curriculum.

11. Students participate as knowledgeable, reflective, creative, and critical members of a variety of literacy communities.

12. Students use spoken, written, and visual language to accomplish their own purposes (e.g., for learning, enjoyment, persuasion, and the exchange of information).

Mary Had a Little Ham: The Poetic Funhouse of Nursery Rhymes

Standards

1. Promotes *reading a wide range of print and nonprint texts* and *learning how the elements of visual language communicate ideas.*
4. Helps students *adjust their language to communicate with different audiences.*
5. Leads writers to *use different writing process elements* (in this case pattern and rhythm) *appropriately; to understand the varying demands of different kinds of writing tasks; and to recognize how to adapt tone, style, and content for the particular task at hand.*
9. Helps students *develop an understanding and respect for diversity in language use, patterns, and dialects across cultures.*
11. Begins to foster a *literacy community* in the classroom.

We live in a serious world. Kids are afraid of getting snatched while walking to school. They have troubles at home. They have seen piles of dead, dismembered bodies on their televisions and video-game screens. There are many somber and heart-wrenching reasons to write poetry. That said, I cannot envision a successful classroom writing experience that begins, "Okay, writers, today we are going to write about depression. Take out a piece of paper." Writing is risky enough; a writer has to ease into these subjects. Also, we shouldn't feel so self-conscious about bringing joy into our classrooms as a means of learning. So let's start out in Bozo shoes and see where they take us.

I like to introduce the concept of pattern in poetry with nursery rhymes. (I can hear the academics now: *Holy cows-over-the-moon! Recreating nursery rhymes? We are trying to get kids beyond nursery rhymes. What in the name of Mother Goose is she talking about? Who needs more nursery rhymes!*)

I warned you: I teach poetry the way I learned it. When I took my one and only creative writing class in college, professor Lyle Crist, my best writing coach in all my years of schooling, started us out rewriting nursery rhymes. It was an effective, memorable lesson that taught me a little about creativity, a lot about patterns and how they work. It was fun and much less intimidating than writing about self-pity and depression (which of course we were all itching to write about). We shared our creations in class the next day, thereby experiencing the power of language as we heard people laugh at our words. We learned how to work-shop, and we relaxed a little about the idea of poetry. Sharing those dopey, silly rhymes helped build a little community in our classroom.

◆ Have students check some nursery rhyme books out of the library as a refresher. This is especially important for the more advanced students. (And nursery rhymes are not just the product of the British Isles. Be sure they include some children's rhymes from other cultures.)

◆ Ask students to rewrite a number of these rhymes.

◆ Let students share their rhymes. Sharing in class is fun, but how about with the first-grade class down the hall? This can lead to a discussion of writing for a particular audience.

◆ Assess students' ability to recognize patterns and rhythms in language and to work as a member of a literacy community.

Something like this works:

> Jack be nimble,
> Jack be quick.
> Get out of the car
> If you're going to be sick.

Something like this doesn't:

> Jack be nimble,
> Jack be quick.
> Please don't take so long as you emerge from the car
> If you feel yourself starting to be sick.

Discuss why.

Here are some student samples from Katie's class at Bay Village Middle School:

It's raining, it's pouring
The tiny old man is boring
We were playing tennis
In the house
And he fell asleep snoring.
—Olivia, Grade 6

Hey diddle, diddle
The girl at Bay Middle
The horse jumped over the hill
The big cat cried
To see he was short
And the sink had to stay in the room.
—Lauren, Grade 6

Jack be nimble, Jack be quick
Jack jumped over a candlestick
If he jumped a little higher
He wouldn't have caught
His pants on fire.
—Jake, Grade 6

Standards

1. Introduces a *range of spoken texts*, providing an opportunity to *study and create visual images.*
2. Helps students *connect sounds to words* and enjoy the musical, *rhythmic qualities of language.*
3. Builds students' knowledge of *word identification strategies* through rhyme.
4. Causes students to *adjust their use of spoke, written, and visual language.*
5. Employs a *process approach to writing,* including *planning, drafting, revising, and editing.*
11. Encourages students to participate *as creative and critical members of a literacy community.*
12. Encourages students to use *visual language* to accomplish their own purposes.

What You Got in That Box?

I was speaking at Fremd High School in Pallantine, Illinois, last spring and a high school junior came up to me after the presentation: "I know you. You came to my elementary school in Northbrook when I was in fifth."

"I did?"

"You did. I know you did. You taught us how to write poetry. No one ever taught us that before. And after that, my friend and I, we started writing poems. We wrote a whole book of poems. It was so much fun. I'm still writing poems."

I grabbed her in a big hug. I didn't even ask permission first (which I usually do), I was so excited.

This is the exercise I used with those fifth graders to get them writing. (*Warning!* It involves rhyme: That old-fashioned pattern that kids still like and we keep telling them is not only unnecessary but something they should feel guilty about, like sugary cereals and getting mud on their clothes.) It teaches or reinforces the writing process: brainstorming, focusing, choosing specific language, organizing one's thoughts, writing, revising, and finally presenting one's ideas orally. And all from the junk (including that black gook in the corners) that you can find in a bathtub. Such a bargain! (A note to the serious teachers of serious students who are conscientiously working with their students to create serious poetry—resist the urge to skip this part. Writing poetry is risky business: Think of this as a trick to get kids used to taking risks in their writing. Especially the serious ones.)

Writing as a Group

◆ Focusing: Begin by helping writers into the bathtub. Put your feet right there. There is a boundary—the edge of the tub. No fair walking down the hall to get a towel or over to the (oh, *no*) toilet. Stay in the bathtub.

◆ Prewriting: Brainstorm a list of details about the bathtub. Not the perfect bathtubs on TV with little scrubbing bubbles running around. Rip back the shower curtain, look for the come-as-you-are truth. Don't spend more than three minutes. Brainstorming is like priming the engine on the lawn mower— a little is a good thing. Flood the engine and you ain't goin' nowhere. It's a grocery list, quick and to the point, like this:

<table>
<tr><td>shower</td></tr>
<tr><td>mat</td></tr>
<tr><td>drain</td></tr>
<tr><td>water</td></tr>
<tr><td>rubber ducky</td></tr>
<tr><td>shampoo</td></tr>
<tr><td>conditioner</td></tr>
<tr><td>curtain</td></tr>
<tr><td>washcloth</td></tr>
<tr><td>Barbie doll</td></tr>
<tr><td>razor</td></tr>
<tr><td>dinosaur</td></tr>
<tr><td>bucket</td></tr>
<tr><td>squirt gun</td></tr>
<tr><td>slippery</td></tr>
<tr><td>hair</td></tr>
</table>

FIG. 2–1 *Brainstorm Bathtub Words*

Oops. Don't forget the soap! Specifics are important. If you want to write humor, you need specifics. "I was in the

> Poetry is to verse
> as love is to affection,
> both a welcome
> comforter
> on long December nights,
> but only one
> presumes
> to warm the heart.
>
> —SARA HOLBROOK,
> *By Definition*

bathtub with some toys" isn't funny. "I was in the bathtub with a dinosaur, Big Bird, and a squirt gun" starts to get funny. Specific words are the building blocks of imagery—what the standards call *visual language*.

◆ More prewriting: Choose a few of the words and create a web of rhyming words. This is (a) fun, (b) a good way to stretch for new words, and (c) an excellent way to get the creative flow started.

◆ Urge kids to think of a logical way to use the rhyming words. For instance, *drain* rhymes with *pain*. Poems are made up of real moments. Have them think of some real moments when they experienced pain in the bathtub or shower (rinsing their hair and hitting their head on the faucet, slipping in spilled shampoo and falling down, turning the water up too hot, getting soap in their eyes).

◆ Make rhyming word groups around only five or six words. Don't overwork it.

◆ Point out that beginning writers often compose poems that slavishly recreate the word groups: *the cat is a rat that sat on a hat and started to chat.* Explain that rhyming word groups are one step in writing lyrical poems (I've even legitimized this product; I call it a Rhyming Word Group—pretty ingenious, huh?), but that to really make a poem, they need to take the next step.

◆ The class will be giggling now. Exchanging ideas. There will be a little chaos as all of these rhyming words start to generate memories and creative ideas: *what if . . . remember when . . . I'll never forget . . . one time. . . .* This chaos is a macrocosm of what happens in the writer's head when a dribble of an idea turns into a downpour. There is only one thing to do. Start writing a group poem before all those great ideas go down the drain.

◆ Refocus: Feet back in the bathtub. No *once upon a time in the backyard I thought about taking a bath* or *it was a dark and stormy night*. Save that for a story. A poem is a snapshot.

- Begin writing with a nonrhyming statement volunteered by one of the students, or combine two ideas. The first line is simply an observation, like a topic sentence: *I stepped into the tub.* No rhymes in the first line! Good.

- Go down to the next line and add another observation. Keep the focus, no rhymes. Don't think like a poem. Think like a journalist: *The water was roaring from the tap.* Great.

- New line. Another observation (*no rhymes;* this trick gets your writers to include three specific observations before they even think about a pattern): *The water was popsicle cold.* Cool.

- Now, have writers underline the last word in the second (middle) statement. This is the key word. We are going to try to put our details in a pattern now, which is what a lot of poetry does. Keep emphasizing that this is only *one* pattern among (roughly) a gazillion. We are creating a poem in an *abcb* rhyme pattern.

- Add a fourth line that rhymes with the second line.

- Save this group poem (and the bathtub poems the kids write as individuals) for a later exercise in revision.

- Assess student participation in group writing process.

The following are some examples of poems kids have written as a result of this exercise.

I stepped into the tub
The water was roaring from the tap.
The water was popsicle cold.
So I tried to adapt.

I put on some mittens.
And socks for my feet.
I stood on a boat
And turned up the heat.

—Sixth Grade,
Orchard Middle School, Solon, Ohio

One day in the bathtub
I was shot by a squirt gun.
I tripped on my duck
    and broke my leg—
It was not fun!

I reached for the curtain rod
and Mom's pantihose.
I fell on my head
And broke my nose.

—Fourth Grade,
Dover Avenue Elementary,
Dover, Ohio

Taking a bath is a process. If you are working with primary grades, students who are limited English speakers, or students with limited academic skills, it is better to write about a *thing*— a lone wolf, a merry-go-round, or a free-tail bat.

Here's another example of the lyrical poem exercise, this time working from the image of a snowman (a bat or a goldfish works just as well). We cataloged words about a snowman. A real snowman. We shook that image of Frosty out of our heads to clarify our thinking and envisioned a crooked snowman in a baseball hat with grass clippings sticking out. After the brainstorm and the rhyming, I asked, "So what's it like for a snowman?" Here's what a class of third graders came up with: *My snowman has no parents*. "No parents?" I asked. "Where'd he come from?" *He comes from snowflakes in the sky*. "Wow. What would that be like—no parents?" One voice responded: *No one yells at him*. The final version of the class poem read:

> My snowman has no parents.
> He comes from snowflakes in the sky.
> No one yells at him,
> Sometimes I wonder why
> he came to earth in my backyard.
> Smoking his pipe
> and standing on guard.
> —Third Grade,
> Dover Avenue Elementary,
> Dover, Ohio

What we've created is a picture with words, aka visual language. This is the test of a good poem. The test is not does it rhyme or not rhyme, but does the poem create an image in the reader's mind?

So, here's the big question. When you read these poems . . . can you picture them? Sure. Are the poems going to win a Pulitzer? No. Have we picked up some tips that will help students hone writing skills. Yes! And we've had some fun in the process.

Writing as Individuals

◆ Walk students through composing their own verses independently, one line at a time. If you just turn them loose, many will recreate the rhyming word groups. Others will start staring at the wall, steam coming out of their ears, trying to noodle out the entire verse before they start to write. That's too hard. You know how I wrote all those books of poetry? One line at a time. Plain and simple. Start there. Still there will be questions:

Teacher! Do I have to write about the bathtub?
> Yes, this is a lesson in focus. Practice your focus with your feet in the tub. Later you can dry off and take the lesson somewhere else. For now, you have a choice. You can continue with the bathtub poem we have all created on the board or you can start your own.

Teacher! I can't think of a first line.
> See this grocery list of words we made about the bathtub? That is your cheat sheet. Just choose a word and put it in a statement. Put *shampoo* or *rubber ducky* in a sentence and start there. Do you hate to take a bath? Start there. Don't overthink it.

Teacher! Teacher! I ended my second line with orange and I can't think of a rhyme.
> Okay, here's the inside scoop. If you cannot rhyme the last word in the second line, just rearrange the lines: Put them in a different order and choose a different word to rhyme. Writing poetry is not skydiving. You don't have to get it right the first time. Think of the lines of the poem as Legos: Move them around until they snap together right.

Here are some samples from Katie's sixth graders. As you read them, ask yourself if you can picture the action. Remember, the goal is to help the kids create visual language by using specifics and putting their ideas in a pattern:

I was in the tub when it happened
A naked Barbie Doll fell right
    on me
Its arms were stretched out wide
I heard the door slam. Where
    was the key?

—Allie

When I got in the tub
My sister didn't care.
She got a bucket of cold water
and dumped it on my hair.

—Kelsey

◆ Reinforce the lesson: After kids have written their own verses, have them share with one another in pairs. No fair just passing their partners the poems; they have to play their words out loud to get the rhythm of them. There will be some frantic erasing and scratching out during this process. This is stage one revision: They see they've dropped a word, used the same word three times, or gotten the rhythm wrong. It is a beginner lesson in the value of reworking. Tell your students this and compliment them. Change is good.

◆ Point out that they did not know the ending of the poem when they started. Sometimes kids struggle with their poetry, making it so much more difficult than prose. Mostly, this is because they are trying to keep the whole poem in their heads while they noodle it out. Tell them: *Don't work that hard*. Write the poem one line at a time and then go back and make changes.

◆ Reinforce the phrase "writing system." They are not just learning how to write dumb ol' bathtub poems. It's okay to be silly, but that would be downright goofy. They are learning a system so that they can use it to write about what they want to write about.

◆ What if they were to use this system to write a poem about a baseball game? What do they need on the list? In twenty seconds they will tell you a ball, a bat, bases, umpire, mitt, hot dogs. That's enough to start writing. This process takes seconds, not hours.

◆ Finally, ask the magic question: Can they think of something in their lives they could make a list about and then turn that list into a poem? Yeah? Like what?

> soccer
> the junk in my backpack
> school lunches
> my dopey brother
> my cat
> walking to school

A suggestion, such as *pets,* is a good point at which to reinforce the concept of narrowing the focus. "Pets" might be a good idea, but there's a world of difference between a gerbil and a canary. If the writer were to write a book of poems about pets, which kind of pet would he start with? Kids need to be reminded over and over to focus their poems on one thing at a time.

◆ Assess students' understanding of the poetry writing process: focusing, prewriting, writing with a focused attention to detail, putting details in a pattern (even if they create their own pattern), and sharing their writing as a literacy community.

The cool thing about creating silly poems in class is that kids are less resistant to ripping them apart for revision. The poems turn into fragrance-free dissecting frogs, able to be torn apart without injury to self or others. I don't know about you, but I have had limited (read zero) success in beginning talks on poetry revision with poems kids have written on topics close to their hearts. So, have the kids hang onto their bathtub poems, but set them aside (in formaldehyde or something) for the moment.

Seventh-grader Dave wrote this poem immediately after we completed a bathtub poem on one of those magic days when I had a group of writers for a double class period. It's important to remember he learned the writing system in a silly way, because his poem is about as far from silly as any kid can get.

> Oh the Pain and Loneliness of that first night.
> As they argued and yelled.
> Then the sadness of the move
> And the hurt as the tears swelled.
>
> No one seemed to care how I felt
> They would go on with their lives with no sadness.
> I'd crie during those nights
> And feel it was my fault for their badness.
>
> The pain I felt could not be shared.
> The teachers just added to my pain.
> And the hurt and mixed feelings
> Most of the time I felt just insane.

Had I had a third period with Dave, we might have identified key words in his poem and maybe experimented with taking the rhyme out. Then again, maybe not. Clearly, this was a deeply heartfelt piece, which means it is *not* an ideal model to break up and reassemble. Just as you don't learn to sew by ripping your grandmother's wedding dress to shreds or learn about the layers applied to the Mona Lisa by peeling them off, some poems just are too dear for kids to dissect. Clearly Dave has more to learn about the art of poetry, and I believe he will. There are lots of models to use to show him these writing lessons. And if he is to become a skilled writer, he will have to produce hundreds of poems. One day he may wish to return to this poem and take a red pen to it. However, I would never ever take a red pen to a poem such as this. Never.

Painless Surgery: The Ongoing Process of Revision

Revision is not something to be saved for last. At its best, revision is ongoing throughout the writing process, from narrowing our focus to weighing and prioritizing material to removing the blemishes and putting the final flush on a manuscript's cheeks. In other words, it's a good thing, not, as a kid once told me, "where you tear up what you wrote and ruin it to make the teacher happy."

We *want* kids to move beyond nursery rhyme patterns. Now that we have helped them put their ideas into a rhyming pattern, we can examine what happens when we take the rhyme out during revision. I have had limited success (read: zero) asking kids to revise poems they wrote on their own and even less success asking them to cut out unnecessary words. If they wrote it, it's necessary. Right? Of course not. But that's where we start as writers. Everything we commit to paper is pure gold. After all these years, cutting my own writing is still a challenge.

This is a revising exercise I cooked up that does work with kids. We're going to help Carl Sandburg with his writing, see if we can punch one of his poems up a little—add a few more words and make his image clearer.

"The Fog" was a very big poem in Pennsylvania a couple of years back. It was on the proficiency tests. Kids were asked to explain what the poem means. I've used the poem in numerous teacher workshops, and you should see the panic that question inspires in grown, educated people. Everyone freezes. *Is there something in there I don't see? Can it be that simple?* Yes, it can. The fog behaves like a little cat. That's it.

That's the trick of good poetry. It's simple. But how do we get to this simple place?

◆ Have the class read Sandburg's "The Fog"—just twenty-one words—and discuss what it means.

◆ Ask students to rewrite the poem, using good figurative language, sharing some additional ways the fog can be like a little cat. Tell them to aim for forty-five words or more. Here are two different approaches from Katie's class. The first (sixty-two words) looks a lot like a poem:

Fog

The fog comes
on little cat feet.

It sits looking
over harbor and city
on silent haunches
and then moves on.

—CARL SANDBURG

The silent fast-moving fog comes in
On the quiet little cat feet looking where to go
It sits looking over for a place to stay
Perhaps the harbor and city will let it in
It stays there on its haunches
Until once again the cat comes to get up and move on
Silently in the shadows of night
Never looking back again.

—Hector, Grade 6

The next takes the shape of a short, eighty-word expository essay:

The hazy gray fog comes as though it was a little lazy cat on little, slow feet finding someplace to sleep. It sits waiting to see if it is comfortable while looking over a harbor and city on its haunches. After a while the cat dozes, of course that's when the fog is heavy and you can't see where you are going. After a while the sun and cat awake, but the sun stays and the cat moves on.

—Hannah, Grade 6

◆ Have students share their work with a partner and then have a few of them read theirs aloud. Comment on the good descriptive language and how the students are attempting to paint a picture with words.

◆ Go back to Carl Sandburg's poem. We don't know what his first draft looked like, but we can be pretty sure it was different from the final twenty-one words. "The Fog" probably started out as an observation, a note on the back of an envelope, a journal entry in prose. From this he was able to find the poem by winnowing the words down to the most essential.

◆ Assess students' ability to rewrite the short poem into a more detailed short essay, capturing the image and expanding on it and appreciating the difference between prose and poetry.

Breaking Out of the Box: Remodeling the Bathtub

Revising poems is volunteering for amputation without an aesthetic. It is scary, can involve major bloodletting, and requires several subsequent transfusions of self-esteem. The reality is that even when we have the kindest, most well-meaning intentions and agonize over word choices, sometimes students *feel* as if they have been cut to pieces. This is why students need to learn the value of self-editing.

◆ Go back to the group poem about the bathtub (or whatever). They wrote it as a group and are going to revise it as a group, in two ways. First, take out as many words as possible and still retain the pattern. Second, abandon the pattern and make free verse out of it. Remember Orchard Middle School's poem?

> I stepped into the tub
> The water was roaring from the tap
> The water was popsicle cold
> So I tried to adapt.
>
> I put on some mittens
> And socks on my feet
> I stood on a boat
> And turned up the heat.
> (42 words)

Cutting out excess words shortens the poem by a third and still retains the *abcb* pattern—and the image:

> Stepped in the tub,
> Water roaring from tap,
> Popsicle cold.
> I tried to adapt.
>
> Mittens on hands,
> Socks on my feet,
> Stood on a boat,
> Turned up the heat.
> (29 words)

1. Demonstrates how *the elements of visual language communicate ideas.*
2. Develops *vocabulary skills* and incorporates *literary language, rich with metaphor, imagery, and other figures and devices.*
3. Draws on students' *knowledge of word meanings and language structure by encouraging them to create meaning in their* writing by imbedding their own *context clues to define* words. Incorporates another *strategy for comprehension, interpreting, and analyzing spoken and visual language.*
4. Draws on students' *knowledge of language conventions (style, vocabulary),* expanding their knowledge of *standard English.*
5. Uses the *writing process elements, including research, prewriting, composition, and presentation.*
6. Affords students the opportunity to *apply their knowledge of language structure and figurative language,* enabling them to work together to *expand their repertoire of syntactic and verbal styles.* Additionally, as students *connect the study of grammar and language to the wider purposes of communication*

Losing the rhyme cuts the poem almost in half and still retains the visual language:

> In the tub
> Water roaring
> Popsicle cold
> Adapt! Adapt!
>
> On with mittens
> On with socks
> Stand in a boat
> Turn up the heat.
> (23 words)

◆ Let the students do the surgery. Make a joke of it: Be ruthless with this poor, defenseless little poem. Take no prisoners. Slash and burn.

◆ You now have three versions of the same poem. Talk about them. Which do they like better? Might a fourth version be even better? Even those who stick to the first version will, if pressed, admit that it could lose a few words.

◆ Have kids drag out their own bathtub poems and repeat the process.

◆ Have them share their revisions with partners and discuss which version works the best and why.

◆ Assess students' ability to condense their work, to clarify an image through revision.

Verb Poems: Action Personified

One of the tricks we use to clarify images is a carefully chosen action verb. Action verbs are the jump and jive of writing, the slip and slide, the . . . you get the picture. No one doubts the efficacy of good verbs in writing; the problem is getting kids to use them instead of *is* and *was*.

Pointing out action verbs in other people's writing is a start, but that's like listening to music on the radio—we know what we like, but that doesn't mean we can duplicate it on our own. We have to handle the instruments, make our own music, strum and toot and pound, in order to appreciate the power of vigorous verbs in writing.

We can raise kids' verb consciousness by letting them examine verbs up close, much the same as we raise environmental consciousness about endangered species by letting kids look at (and perhaps handle) them in zoos. That parallel isn't too far-fetched: Many of these little verb critters, such as *sluice, conjure,* and *swagger,* are indeed endangered. Some scholars claim the average vocabulary is shrinking; others claim the human vocabulary is growing at an amazing rate, with new words being added every day. My experience from reading the poetry of students is that too often their content and images suffer miserably from a case of the "vaguelies," crippled by *you know/whatever/you get my drift* assumptions.

A reader doesn't know anything unless the writer provides it definitively. For this reason, word choice is of crucial importance to writers, especially poets. I have taught myself a lot about the way words work by writing definition poems, mostly defining nouns (see page 33). But by applying the same imaginative vision to verbs, we can enhance students' writing while folding in a lesson on personification.

◆ Share one or more of my verb poems. When I was working in Katie's class, I started with "Run" and then proceeded to "Swagger" and "Vacillate." The kids did not know what *swagger* or *vacillate* meant, but after I read them the poems, they were able to tell me. These are so simple to do, you might scratch one out yourself as a model. (Verb poems can take many different formats, from limericks to haiku.)

and artistic development, they are considerably more likely to incorporate such study into their working knowledge.

7. Encourages *investigation into an issue or problem chosen by the student,* using language *itself as a valuable research tool,* providing students the opportunity to gather, evaluate, and synthesize data from a wide variety of sources (dictionaries, thesaureses).

8. Provides an opportunity for computer-based research and to *use technology to compose texts and graphics.*

Run
is a way to go
that travels lightning fast.
When the Gameboy starts to run
you know the batteries won't last
forever,
you better
catch what starts to run
before
the
opportunity
is
past,
because, run
is a way to go
that travels lightning fast.

—SARA HOLBROOK

Swagger
thinks he's better,
turns his cap toward the back,
curls his lip, refuses to skip
or act like a kid.
Ever.
He's self-assured when he walks in,
full of nerve with a hint of sin,
one hand in his pocket,
with shoulders square,
and if you don't like it, he doesn't care.
Somewhere between a strut and stroll,
he's on a roll, his step in time
to a silent beat that says, "Bring it on,"
'cause he's all that
from his crown to his feet.

—SARA HOLBROOK

Vacillate cannot
make up its mind, up or down,
stay or wait . . . who cares?

—SARA HOLBROOK

Adverbs tag along
while verbs carry the load.
Why just run quickly,
when I can explode?
Who wants to eat sloppily?
I'd rather pig out.
Who wants to speak loudly?
I'd rather shout.
Verbs rock and roll
as they move things along,
the way that a melody carries a song.

—MICHAEL SALINGER/SARA HOLBROOK

◆ Have the kids go on a safari in search of action verbs, maybe even some of the endangered variety, depending on their level of comprehension. Remind them that they can pull out the dictionary and thesaurus.

◆ Ask them to put the verb they've chosen at the top of a paper divided into two columns, labeled *is* and *is not*. Encourage personification by asking, "If this verb were a person, how would it behave? What kinds of things would it like to do? not like to do?" These lists become their cheat sheet when they start to compose verb poems.

◆ Have students share their poems by exchanging papers with one another. Ask them to respond in writing to the poems they have been passed, either by putting the poem into their own words or by using the verb in a sentence. Have either the writer or the responder read the poem out loud, even act it out.

◆ Ask students to create graphic computer-generated illustrations for their poems to further their appreciation for the figurative language their have used in their verb personifications.

◆ Assess students' ability to define an action verb by writing a poem using personification and figurative language, their knowledge of the meaning of the verb, and their ability to respond to another student's poem.

Tackle

Tackle is mean and
really rough

He will never really think
he has enough
He uses his arms, hands,
feet and body
He is really naughty

He will do what he
needs to do
He will hurt you.

—Jacob, Grade 6

Swing

Swing strikes out at home
he blows by the
ball   he's a stroke
a motion   he is a hit
—Mason, Grade 6

Yawn opens her mouth up wide
So you can almost see inside.
When you wake yawn comes by
But do you ever wonder why?
She likes sleepiness and boredom,
   too.
When you stretch, she'll come to
   you.
Energetic is never her
Mood, but
She never keeps her mouth shut.
—Halle, Grade 6

FIG. 2–2 *Verb Poem "Yawn"*

One student took up my challenge to find an extinct verb.

Standards

1. Causes students to *predict*, and *think about what happens next, how characters feel,* and *why an author makes choices.* Further, it helps raise students' awareness that *any given text can be understood in a variety of ways.*
2. Teaches students that *literary texts are often relevant to their own lives* and helps them *make connections,* affording them the opportunity to *engage in ethical and philosophical reflection* that leads to *the development of critical thinking skills.*
3. Teaches students that *reading is an active, recursive process in which readers make predictions based on linguistic and contextual clues (including the reader's knowledge of the world) and reevaluate those predictions in light of other cues, causing* students to *move from predicting to confirming (or revising) their predictions and back again. Thoughtful attention to their own cognitive processes will be rewarded with more complete and meaningful reading experiences and with an explicit sense of how to manage their own thinking.*

Flout

She disobeys her
parents.
She is very rude
and mean.
She always says
insults.
And isn't very
clean.
She gets grounded
all the time.
She never
listens.
She misbehaves
and never shaves.
She pouts
and isn't very nice.

—Katie, Grade 6

And the Inference Is . . .

Inference is big in the English language arts standards. Well, it isn't exactly stated in that way, but words such as *predicting, revising, context clues,* and *connections* are all over the standards, which leads me to *infer* that inference is a big deal. Ginger Weincek, a third-grade teacher in Elgin (Illinois) School District U4, works to improve her students' reading skills by teaching inference through poetry. Here's the lesson she constructed using one of my poems. Ginger's lesson translates well into introducing complicated, sometimes somewhat obscure poetry in the upper grades. I'll let Ginger set this up in her own words:

I read to my kids every day after lunch—probably close to twenty-five minutes. It seems like it takes *forever* to get through a book because of all the talking we do each day. In the beginning of the year, I am the one doing most of the talking. I model my own thinking very explicitly, but naturally. I'll put the book down on my lap and say, "I'm thinking this really means thus-and-so," for example, or muse, "I wonder if the author is suggesting such-and-such." I make sure to emphasize whatever strategy we are focusing on at the time, but include other strategies as well so they can see how a proficient reader thinks. Then I pick up the book and continue. As the year progresses, I invite them to join me in thinking aloud. Of course some kids become peer models for those who aren't as comfortable with the concept. But when I start having them turn to a partner to share their thinking (or a connection, or a question, or a sensory image), everyone actively participates. The strategies are the *how* of our thinking but good readers think using whatever strategy fits that text and their own need at the time.

◆ Choose a poem like "Doubt" that challenges your students to make predictions and connections to their own lives.

◆ Reveal one stanza of the poem at a time, asking the kids at each step to predict what may be happening in the poem. Here are some things Ginger's kids wondered:

About the title, "Doubt":

> I wonder if this poem will tell us what *doubt* is?
> I wonder if this poem is about a parent doubting a kid?
> I wonder if this poem is about a kid doubting a lot of things?
> I wonder if this poem is about someone getting mad?

About the first stanza:

> I wonder if the *lace* stands for losing your trust?
> I wonder if something bad happened to him?
> I wonder if the kid gets mad at himself sometimes?
> I wonder if he hurts himself inside?
> I wonder if he falls down in life?
> I wonder if he falls behind in the race because he doubts he can win?

Doubt

Insecure
Is a lace untied
That in a race
Trips me
Inside.
It hints that I don't have
    the stuff.
Why try when I'm not
    good enough?

And once I stumble
In my mind
It's harder not to
Fall behind.

It sure would be
A faster route
If I could live
Without a doubt.

—SARA HOLBROOK,
By Definition

About second stanza:

> I wonder if he thinks he's not good enough?
> I wonder if he's doubting that he can't do what he is trying
>   to do?
> I wonder if he's not going to try because he is not good?
> I wonder if he doesn't know what to do when he has a
>   problem?
> I wonder if he is going to just give up?

About the last stanza:

> I wonder if he is running from his mind?
> I wonder what "I could live without a doubt" means?
> I wonder is the *race* going through life and he'd do better if
>   he didn't doubt himself?
> I wonder is he racing through his mind?

And here are some of the inferences Ginger's kids made:

- I think that the race is going through life. And the untied lace is his or her feelings.
- I think the part that says "in a race trips me inside" means
  that the kid has problems and he can't help himself.
- I think "Insecure is a lace untied that in a race trips me
  inside" means that you're doing something and you're
  tired and you're giving up.
- I think the part where it says "Insecure is a lace untied
  that in a race trips me inside" means that the life he is
  having is not very good so when he doubts something
  he trips and falls in his life but when he believes in himself he stands back up.
- I think that when it says "Insecure is a lace untied that
  in a race trips me inside" it means that he needs to stop
  doubting himself so much because he if he keeps doing
  that that's why he feels like tripping. I think if he keeps

doing that he won't get to the place he wants to be in life.

◆ Based on the students' participation in the literary discussion, assess their abilities to make connections and predict outcomes based on the text.

Write It Out, Don't Act It Out: The Emotions of Poetry

Once after a school visit, a teacher told me she'd been happy to find I wasn't nearly as angry in person as she thought I would be after reading my poetry. I reminded her that when we write about our feelings, we can put them in a book and close the cover; we don't have to carry them around and spit them in people's faces. This exercise looks at the "guts" of emotions—what goes on inside us—some of which naturally spills out to our external selves.

First students write independently, then they combine their poems with partners to create a poem for two voices that compares and contrasts two different emotions. By turning their combined poems into a classroom performance, students learn how to communicate emotions through words, a sure fire way to engage an audience.

To write about emotions, we have to acknowledge that we have them. I know that's a very Dr. Phil comment, but kids are tough. They often don't acknowledge that they have any feelings at all. *Don't care, so what,* and *whatever* are their bywords. Ask your average middle-grade students how they are feeling and you will most likely get one of two responses—*okay* or *ticked off.* They are slower to acknowledge *why* they are ticked off—because they are disappointed, rejected, sad, or impatient. We need to look inside to find physical descriptions to enhance our writing, to "show don't tell."

Angry

I'm angry.
Foot stomping,
door kicking,
wall hitting,
book throwing,
desk slapping,
drawer slamming,
pencil breaking,
teacher hating,
paper tearing,
teeth bearing
mad.

The worst part is,
can't you see?
There's no one else to
    blame
but me.

—SARA HOLBROOK,
Wham, It's a Poetry Jam

4. Draws on students' *knowledge of language conventions* and provides an opportunity to *make sense of how print communicates its message to the audience.*

5. Helps students apply *language conventions and structure;* helps them use *elements of writing flexibly and adaptively* to become *confident and effective writers.*

6. Helps students employ *language conventions, including grammar,* to create *visual text* while fostering an understanding *that attention to structure and form is an essential part of the process of creating and revising text.*

9. Fosters an understanding of the *power of figurative language.*

10. Provides *social interaction,* which is essential for language learning.

11. Builds a literacy community by *creating a community of engaged listeners* with an *interest in the characters and events of the narrative.*

12. Encourages students to use *spoken, written, and visual language for self-expression.*

Part One

◆ Share the poem "Angry" with your students. Cover up the title and the first line and ask if they can guess the emotion this poem conveys.

◆ Point out the noun-participle-noun-participle pattern.

◆ Tell them they are each going to rewrite this little poem after giving it a new title—a different emotion.

◆ Brainstorm some possible emotions—excited, depressed, nervous, lazy, happy, and so on. (This is an essential step, since some of your students won't be that willing to admit that they have any emotions.)

◆ Have students rewrite the poem. It doesn't have to duplicate the rhyme scheme but should reflect the noun-participle pattern.

FIG. 2–3 *Students Writing Verb Poems*

- Ask writers to share their (unlabeled) poems with a partner; can the partner guess the emotion?

- Emphasize that the next time they write a story or poem they may express an emotion by describing a physical response instead of using a label—they can say a person is "tummy jumping" instead of excited or "foot tapping" instead of impatient.

- Assess students' ability to express emotions through actions, follow a pattern in their writing, and participate as performers and listeners in the classroom.

Tired

I'm tried
muscles aching
feet hurting
neck creaking
eyes drooping
brain sleeping
I am tired.
—Adam, Grade 6

Bored

I'm bored
big yawning
eyes slouching
slow blinking
being told
slow doing
want to sleep
want to do something else
feet sleeping
It is very clear
that school rarely has cheer.
　　　　　—Dan, Grade 6

Embarrassed

I'm embarrassed
pants falling
foot tripping
fart smelling
nose picking
hall sliding
voice cracking
chair tipping
mom singing
embarrassed!
How 'bout you?
—Katie Lufkin (teacher)

Part Two

Although there are many good reasons for having a dog or a cat for a pet, there are also factors that allow each animal to distinguish itself in a person's home. How's that for a compare and contrast opener? I wrote it all by myself. I based it on 47.6 (by exact count) school website examples of how to frame a comparison. It's dull as dirt, but it works. I guess.

We want students to be able to recognize and describe similarities and differences between things. But these comparisons need not be convoluted or induce snoring. Collaborating on poems for two voices can help kids toward that goal.

- Begin by modeling a poem for two voices. One is provided on page 160, but many others can be found in your library. (Ask the media specialist. She has a bunch of poetry books that aren't getting the circulation they deserve.)

- Divide the students up in pairs (a group of three is okay too, to round things out).

- Ask students to put their emotion poems together and discuss their differences and similarities. To jump-start a discussion, ask something like, "How might excitement be similar to depression?" (loss of sleep, jumpiness). "How might they be different?" (One is hopeful, one is not).

- Have the pairs of writers construct a poem for two voices that compares and contrasts two emotions through visual and sensory details. Ask them not to state what the emotions are until the end of the poem, thus leading the reader to infer. They should collaborate to write concluding lines or stanzas for their poems that pull the effort together.

- Put together a classroom performance of these poems. Discuss how the comparisons are made through specific detail. (In Katie's sixth-grade class, we had a lot of fun combining and performing our emotion poems for two voices. I encouraged them to act out the poems, to take them over the top. And boy, did they.)

- Assess students' understanding of the compare and contrast concept and their abilities to collaborate and incorporate visual and sensory details into their writing.

Love Struck and Confused

I'm in love
        but confused
Hand shaking
        heart racing
Head twisting
        bad talking
Stomach shaking
        heart breaking
Mind racing
        fingers aching
Foot taping
        feels like floating
Palms sweating
        butterflies twitching
Hair yanking
I'm confused
        but in love
        —Sophie and Melissa,
                Grade 6

Hyper/Lazy

        couch laying
wall bouncing
        chip eating
sugar eating
        TV watching
leg jumping
        remote clicking
loud laughing
        deep sleeping
face smiling
        —Matt and Charlie,
                Grade 6

Embarrassed/Tired

I'm embarrassed
        I'm tired
pants falling
        muscles aching
feet tripping
        feet hurting
nose picking
        neck cracking
voice cracking
        eyes drooping
mom singing
        brain sleeping
I am embarrassed
        I am tired.
We'd rather be
        at home in bed
No more school
        That's what we said.
        —Katie Lufkin and Natalie,
                Grade 6

Images: Writing from the Outside in (Pictures in Something Less Than 1,000 Words, Maybe 849 or 760, Give or Take a Few, If You Can Possibly See What I'm Talking About)

Discussions of imagery in poetry can go on and on. And on. A shame, since part of the point of using an image in a piece of writing is to clarify the message with fewer words. Crayons are still about the most fun a person can have for pennies, which is why it is difficult to explain the current crayon shortage in most middle-grade classrooms. How can we talk about images in writing if we don't have kids draw some pictures, a much more efficient route to understanding? Visualizing is a key component in comprehension. Kids need to see what they are reading and in turn they will be more likely to incorporate visual details in their own writing.

- Ask students to draw a picture of a poem's central image.

- Have students reread the poem several times to make sure that they have the picture in their minds, thereby improving comprehension.

- Or use a picture as a writing prompt. This is one of the most effective ways I know of to get kids to commit words to paper.

- Assess whether the students' pictures (or words) reflect an adequate interpretation of the poem (or picture).

Metaphor: Words + Images = A Blast of Surprise

Substituting one thing for another happens naturally with little kids: Pencils become people in an instant and march up and down coffee tables (and leave little footprints in the wood, much to the frustration of parents). But by the intermediate grades, kids are already editing themselves out of these creative connections. That kind of play is just plain silly, right? Maybe. But it is those silly connections that can inspire our most creative writing. Kids watch reality TV, reality on their street corners, reality movies. They become realistic—sometimes painfully and tediously realistic—and need a shot of metaphor to get them thinking in terms of creative connections.

This rewrite exercise, introduced to me at Crofton House School in Vancouver, BC, Canada, invites the imagination to flow by connecting an emotion to external images through metaphor. The student samples included here were created by Katie's sixth graders in Bay Village, Ohio. An international effort!

- ◆ Introduce the kids to my poem "Disappointment." Discuss.

- ◆ Have the kids rewrite the poem using a different emotion.

- ◆ Assess students' ability to see one thing in terms of another.

Amazed!
What a surprise—
You're a soccer ball out of nowhere.
You're a superhero that can glide.
You're a 15-foot person.
You're a 108-foot slide.
——Joe, Grade 6

Nervous!
What a surprise—
You're spiders crawling up my back.
You're a mess-up from an important play.
You're butterflies in my stomach.
You're the confidence that I lack.
——Christa, Grade 6

Disappointment

Disappointment!
What a surprise—
You're a blast from door's-open cold.
You're nuts in my chocolate cream.
You're a late lunch
        and bread sprouting mold.

Disappointment?
You're a blister from new favorite shoes.
You promised and then you forgot.
You're just crumbs where there
        once was a cake.
You looked honest, but then you were not.

Disappointment—
You took pliers and yanked out my trust
like a dentist without Novocaine,
then you didn't return my calls
when I tried to express my pain.

——SARA HOLBROOK,
By Definition

The Metaphor Reaches over the Top: Bringing It All Together

This three-part exercise can be done in fifty minutes. I get squeezed into that period of time regularly during school residencies. It might be better if you are able to spread this over two class periods, however, giving the students and you more time to write.

You start with an image selected from the newspaper. Students first write as a group, then write individually about a personal topic. The goal is to help students understand how metaphor works by having them build one of their own in a

Standards

All the writing elements mentioned earlier, along with—
12. Integrates knowledge inside and outside the classroom by developing students' *appreciation for their own and others' self-expression,* helping to hone *students' listening skills,* and *strengthening their literacy community.*

group writing exercise, then use this knowledge to build a poem incorporating real images out of personal experiences.

The general topic is "conflict," since it is not only universal but also an element in virtually all stories. Building poems of conflict helps kids identify conflict in stories or poems and leads them to a better understanding of cause and effect, conflict and resolution.

Part One

◆ Choose an article out of a newspaper that describes a conflict of some kind, natural or manmade. (Articles I have used in the past were about a wildfire, a chemical explosion, a volcano, a school bus accident, a hurricane, a war.)

◆ Have one volunteer read from the article in short sound bites while the other students help you catalog a list of key words on the board. You will only have to read a couple paragraphs of the story to come up with twenty or so words.

◆ Tell students they could probably use these words to write a pretty adequate poem on a war or a wildfire or whatever the topic. But poetry comes from real experiences—from places in the heart, not places in a newspaper. Set these words aside for the time being.

Part Two

◆ Create a common experience that might inspire a poem.

◆ Ask for two student volunteers who feel they can act like two macho guys.

◆ Privately tell the actors that their roles will be to walk past one another, bump elbows, and then turn and glare at each other. (You're trying to capture the moment right before a conflict erupts, before that wildfire took off, before the bomb exploded or the hurricane ripped through town, but keep that to yourself.) Explain that they are not really to strike out at each other, but to stare one another down, puff up and set their jaws, *as if* they were going to fight.

♦ Have the two macho guys come back into the classroom and stand on opposite sides of the room at the front of the class.

♦ Instruct the other students to think like journalists as they watch the scene. Alert them to be very aware of what does happen and what does *not* happen between the two guys.

♦ Let the macho guys act out the scene. (Lead the applause and congratulate them on being good sports, then invite them to rejoin the class.)

♦ Ask the class what they saw. Start with who, what, when, where. Who was involved? What really happened? What did *not* happen?

♦ List student responses on the board, in a column separate from the newspaper article words (and in a different color chalk, if you have it). Have the students look at these words. They could undoubtedly write a pretty adequate poem about an almost-fight on the sidewalk or in the hallway using these words.

♦ Then ask, could they write a poem about an almost-fight using the words from the article? Yes? Maybe? Watch the lightbulbs go on. This is metaphor, on a very basic level, taking the words describing one thing and applying them to another.

♦ Using short phrases offered by the students, compose a group one-thing-for-another poem on the board.

♦ Read the poem aloud to the students and ask, "Can you picture that?" Listen for the collective, "Wow."

Fifth graders in Katie's class at Orchard Elementary School in Cleveland, Ohio, applied aspects of an approaching thunderstorm to the almost-fight:

> Two guys circle like a tornado.
> They crash like thunder.
> They get booming mad.
> Eyes pop and flash like lightning.
> No fight.
> No words.
> Just darkness from their mouths.

Katie's sixth-grade class used words from an article about an auto-racing accident:

> Two shoulders crashed in the skidway
> both vehicles halted and turned around
> a quick response time
> caution thrown away
> an explosive scene
> battered egos
> no officials arrive
> but the caution flag is out.

Part Three

From here, the entire class *could* go on to write about an almost-fight in the school hallway. But poetry is more personal than that. Additionally, it's a big turnoff to be told exactly what to write about. It's time for the students to write on their own about something personal to them, using the group poem as a model.

The Prewrite

- Have students take a piece of notebook paper and fold it in half lengthwise, producing a shape similar to a reporter's notebook.

- Remind them that in very general terms they have been writing about conflict, first a conflict (nature, man vs. nature, man vs. man) reported in the newspaper and then a conflict between two pretend macho guys. Speculate that everyone in the classroom has personally experienced some kind of conflict—a conflict with a sibling, with a coach, with a parent over a curfew, with a stubborn lawn mower or computer.

- Ask students to identify a conflict in their lives, either current or when they were little.

- Tell them to focus on a single event. If the chosen conflict is ongoing (one with mom about keeping their bedroom free of litter and vermin), ask them to focus on a particular moment when things came to a head.

- Ask them to make a list of facts about this incident. Encourage them to record details. Start easy with the basic Ws of journalism: Who was involved? What was the issue? Where did this happen, exactly? in the kitchen, the classroom, the parking lot? When? What time of day, time of year?

- Ask them to think about all their senses. Were there any background noises, like television blaring or tires screeching? How about odors or fragrances? What was the light source? candle? florescent? sunny day?

- Have them brainstorm for no more than five or six minutes.

- Ask them if this feeling they have cooking inside of them reminds them of anything else: a hurricane? an explosion? a volcano? the time their bike got swiped? Have them write a few details about this.

It would be oh so handy if there were some kind of cutesy acrostic way to teach people how to write meaningful poetry. There isn't. To write poetry we have to go back into the moment we are writing about and relive it. There are no shortcuts. We have to feel the moment.

The Draft

◆ Have students put their pencils down and open their papers. One side of the unfolded paper will contain their brainstormed list, the other will be blank. That is where they are going to develop their poems, right next to the facts.

◆ Ask them to close or cover their eyes (whatever is comfortable), shut out the outside world, and go back into that moment—feel it, let the experience wash over them. There will be a lot of words swimming around in their heads.

◆ Ask them to visualize the first line of their poems, and when they have it, write it down. Writers will take various amounts of time here; some will have it right off, others will need a few minutes to noodle it out.

◆ Tell them to keep writing for ten minutes or so. If they get blocked, they should review their list and/or go back into the experience and feel the moment. The room will be silent as everyone writes.

The Discussion

◆ Before the bell rings, begin the discussion. Ask students to share, *in very general terms,* the source of their conflict: a sibling thing? a parent thing? a school or friend thing? a mechanical thing? Kids should be open to this kind of general questioning.

◆ Ask students how the writing went. Were they surprised that they could come up with poems that efficiently? What they are doing here is cleansing their palate to be able to look at revision. Talking helps draw them out of the writing, and they can then turn back to the poem with a fresher eye.

The Proofread

◆ Ask students to pair up and share their poems. No fair just passing the other person the poem, say the words out loud.

This is the only way to see if a poem is working or not and uncover basic flaws such as skipped words or repeated phrases. Kids will do this quietly at first, then there will be some laughter and chitchat.

◆ When everyone is finished reading, ask what the laughter is about. Aren't we talking about issues that bothered us? What's so funny? Kids may begin to acknowledge that while the issue they were writing about was serious at the time, now that they look back on it, it's kind of funny. Or they will say it still bothers them but sharing it with another person makes it less serious.

◆ Let them know that the chitchat is important, that what they are doing is workshopping their poetry. Have them think about what they said to their partners. Were they offering further explanation of the poems? If so, that explanation belongs in the poems. A poem must be able to stand on its own two feet when the poet is not there to provide an explanation.

◆ Tell them to jot down at the bottom of the page any important facts they think might belong in their poems.

A pet peeve (only one?): I go to a poetry reading and someone comes up to the microphone, gives a five-minute introduction to the poem, reads a two-minute poem, and then follows up with another five minutes of "what I really meant to say." That poet is workshopping the poem in public. An annoying and distracting habit. I once listened in on a writer who was sharing her poem with her partner. After reading the poem, she remarked, "Now, what you need to know is that I was pregnant at the time and really off balance." This is an important detail, it belongs in the poem, not in the imaginary footnotes!

The Revision

◆ Have everyone title their poem the same: version 1.

◆ Have them pull out another piece of paper and label that version 2.

◆ Ask students to count the words in version 1 and write that number in the margin. (Do not bend, destroy, or mutilate version 1.)

◆ Tell students to create version 2, a condensed rendering of version 1 with about one-third fewer words. They can accomplish this by making a list of the key words in version 1 or eliminating unnecessary words. (If they used a rhyming pattern in version 1, they may want to experiment with taking out the rhyme.) Whatever the approach, version 2 is to be a slimmer poem.

◆ Reiterate that both version 1 and version 2 belong to the poet; ultimately it is the poet's decision which is working better.

◆ Ask whether anyone likes version 2 better than version 1. Some will remain true to version 1, others will acknowledge that cutting out some of the words was a positive thing.

◆ Have a few volunteers share both of their versions with the class and explain which version is working better for them and why. Ultimately, most will agree that what works best would actually be a third version somewhere in between the two original poems.

◆ Assess students' ability to build a visual image in a poem using imagery and metaphorical connections.

Student Writing Samples

Dwayne, age 10, and in the fifth grade at Orchard Elementary School in Cleveland, Ohio, was having some problems with the driver of his school bus.

Dwayne's Brainstormed List

mad

not fair

steamy

eye squinting

loud

foot stumping [*sic*]

fist

got headache

smacked lips

no punching

no fight

no hitting

no words

no happiness

Bus Driver (first draft)

I'm mad.
I'm so mad.
I roared like a lion, I wasn't
lien [*sic*]. I couldn't
start crying
when the bus
driver said whate [*sic*],
I said, I'll do it tonight.
I made a fist,
then came a headache,
everything was just
mist, fog. I was steamy.
I was hot, but there was
one thing I didn't want to admit,
it was all my fault.

This poem appears to have led to a little insight on Dwayne's part. Poetry does that. Naturally Dwayne's poem could benefit from some revision (his tenses are a bit confused, spelling is hit-and-miss), but as first drafts from fifth graders go, Dwayne has done a good job of capturing the intensity of the moment.

Next is the work of Michael, age 12, Columbia Station, Ohio.

Michael's Brainstormed List

stronger

football field

fall

cool breeze

orange leaves

crouched

one hand on the groin

bursting

charging

adrenalin

contact

Michael's Poem

Out of the huddle
we gather on the line
a cool fall breeze
whips past our helmets
crouching down
awaiting the motion.
I stare hard
awaiting the strike
loathing the opponent
only worry about the ball.
It moves
teams collide like great armies

exploding, flying back
running
chasing
diving
rolling
kicking

utter chaos
and yet total order.
I turn for the play
running down among my
comrades
the mission must be
completed.
I see him
eye contact is made
I move for the kill
Adrenalin pumping
waiting for the moment
I dive and wrap as he
tries to avoid my grip
sliding along the wet ground.
I land in a heap
but without the boy
my heart sinks.
I get up
there he is lying
success!

What I like about both Michael's and Dwayne's poems is the attention to physical detail. Both incorporate one simile as they reach for comparisons to clarify their poems. Remember when assessing poems such as these that the kids are learning the building blocks of good writing. While everything might not stack up in perfect balance at first, it's important to acknowledge that the writer is beginning to reach for the right blocks.

Eighth-grader José's poem has a strong hip-hop influence, but he has not limited himself by rhyme, providing a clear, emotional image that incorporates sounds and shadows. José worked very hard to include all the details of his brainstorm in his poem and then said to me privately, "I worked it all in except for this"—he pointed to the phrase "broken home." I suggested it might make a good title. He nodded solemnly and penciled it in.

Broken Home

She's always yelling,
afraid of telling.
There's always something, I start
regretting, so I started to run.
This is not fun.
I got to hide, trying not to cry.
I'm all alone
in the shadows,
listening to the
soothing sound
of raindrops.

I try to work things out
in my mind.
There's some kind of pain.
There's a huge stain
I can't contain
within my family,
I cannot tame.

The following poem was written by a teacher who participated as a full member of his class' writing community. It demonstrates the power of teacher engagement. As you read it, ask yourself if you can put a grade on the value of sharing it with the class. My rough estimate is: priceless.

Rain slashing the sky
As black-grey clouds shed their tears.
The open hole swallows my father wholly;
Eighty-three years buried beneath the clay.
My mother weeps silently,
Her loneliness breaks the silence of
The country graveyard minutes
Before the long drive home to the
Empty house where his shade sits
In his favorite chair snoring.

—James Claffey
Gompers Secondary School

Nobody Listens to Me: Publication

Emily Dickinson told us that publication is the "auction of the soul," and writers step up on the block with relentless insistence: What they want (some of them more than they want to write, which is disheartening) is to find an audience. Providing an audience for student writing is just as important as the brainstorm and the draft, maybe more so. Knowing that someone else will ultimately read or hear them is both an inspiration and a reason for taking revision a little more seriously. No writing lesson plan is complete until you have answered the question, *What do I do with these poems after the kids have written them?* (Hint: The answer is not to take them home in a spiral-frayed pile to clutter up your weekend.)

Some Suggestions

◆ Create a class literary journal complete with student artwork. This will cost you big time in terms of money and effort, but the rewards (and sometimes state prizes) can make the process more than worthwhile.

◆ Create an online journal that parents and friends can access from home. If you don't have the computer skills, guaranteed there's a little hacker in one of your classes who does.

◆ Buy some chunky chalk and let students have at it on the front sidewalk.

◆ Invite another class in to a poetry reading or move the reading outside the school, to a Kiwanis luncheon or your local bookstore.

◆ Invite parents to an evening reading. (While you're at it, invite parents to bring their poems in, too. There's some great stuff out there. It will do a lot to foster a literacy community beyond your classroom and to show students that this writing thing need not be confined to school.)

- Have students submit poems to local newspapers, arts magazines, church newsletters, and student publications, even publications that don't usually publish poetry.

- Have students make submissions to national publications such as *Teen Ink*. (*Word of caution:* There are some disreputable organizations out there taking poetry from kids in exchange for lots of $$. I would advise avoiding the National Poetry Library all together and other for-profit organizations promising poetry prizes. The prize is usually a hefty bill for the book.)

- Call up the local cable company and ask what they are doing to promote literacy in your community. The FCC says they should be doing something. Maybe they want to film some of your poets for broadcast.

- Create a video journal of students reading their poetry and see if you can air it on your school's announcement monitors. (Don't have video announcements? How about reading a poem a week over the squawk box?)

- Have kids publish their own chapbooks. Reputable poets like Whitman, Poe, Frost, and (ah-hem) me started out self-publishing. It is a time-honored traditional stepping-stone for many.

- Investigate writing contests in your area and have kids submit entries. Nominal reading fees may apply ($5 to $10; the money is used to pay—about two cents an hour—the folks who handle the submissions). If funds are short, have the kids sell some candy bars at lunch or something; it will be a real encounter with the joys and challenges of the literary life. (Having them skip a few meals and sleep on a friend's sofa or an airport floor would also be an insight into the real literary life, but you needn't go that far. Too much reality might be discouraging to burgeoning writers.)

> "The Joy that isn't shared,
> I've heard dies young."
>
> —ANNE SEXTON

◆ Have kids share their poems with peers and perform them in class. If you are looking for suggestions on how to get kids out of their seats and improve their oral presentation skills, check out my book *Wham, It's a Poetry Jam*. About that word *performance*. I am a performance poet by trade and as such have endured the subtle slings and arrows of those who wish to put us in a separate-but-not-equal category from other poets. Spoken-word poetry can in fact be dreadful, but no more dreadful than the work of some poets who only commit themselves to the page. Also, any time we clear our throats to talk to more than two others, that's a performance, and we have a choice about whether we mumble our way through it or speak with conviction and emotion. The national standards, and all the state standards, I reviewed list: develop the ability of students to express themselves with clarity. Performing poetry can help achieve this goal.

A Poet's Self-Edit Checklist

1. *Have I written from one pair of shoes?* Often first drafts appear to be speaking from more than one perspective, perhaps beginning in first person, switching midstream to second person, and ending up in some philosophical third-person summary (*I hate anchovies/Anchovies make you sick/Anchovies are stinko*). Check that the poem has only one point of view.

2. *Have I narrowed the focus?* If I have chosen to write about a larger issue (love, war, death, the environment), have I tried to narrow the focus to one moment? Broad poems can divide like amoebas into clear, sharp images when the poet narrows the focus.

3. *Have I defined all of my opinion words (aka subjective terms)?* Words, such as *weird, gorgeous, lovely, lively, crazy,* and so on, all need to be defined in concrete terms so that the reader can visualize the poet's image. *Crazy* as

what? *Gorgeous* because? Does my poem describe the sunset in such a way that I don't have to even say it was gorgeous—did I show rather than tell?

4. *Have I double-checked the basics?* Subject-verb agreement? Present, future, or past tense (choose one)? Spelling?

5. *Have I worked to get the trite out?* Get rid of phrases and aphorisms that are so common that they have lost their meaning in concrete terms: *cold as ice, screamed like a hyena, beauty is as beauty does.* Such phrases are annoying enough when Mom uses them and even worse in poetry. What does the phrase really mean—can I reword it in an original way?

6. *Have I practiced cutting out excess words?* What happens if I arbitrarily delete one-quarter or one-third of the words? Poetry is economical communication; am I saving wherever possible?

7. *Have I read the poem aloud to see if it flows and makes sense?* Yea, verily, thy convoluted language shall be stricken! Talk the poem out—ask, Is this something I would say or my narrator would say?

8. *Does the poem contain any fake rhymes?* A fake rhyme is like a fake smile—anyone can spot a phoney. A rhyme that was chosen for rhyme's sake, not the sake of the message (The ocean is my storage tank/Where I go to fish with Hank), makes for a weak poem. Can I rearrange the poem to get rid of forced, fake, or too predictable rhymes?

9. *Have I used action verbs to clarify images?* Can I substitute verbs that move for words like *is, are, went, came,* and so on?

10. *Was I consistent to the pattern I chose?* A lot of poetry is about putting details into a pattern. Patterns should

remain consistent as they play in the background of the poem. If the pattern breaks in one point, it will draw the focus of the reader to that broken place. Writers break a pattern in the middle of a poem only if the purpose is to attract the readers' attention.

11. *Did I maintain a clear and consistent image?* Were descriptive words used, including comparisons such as simile and metaphor? This is the poetic version of a home run: Can the reader picture what is in the poem? Let the poem cool off overnight, look at it again with the eyes of a stranger, and ask, Can I picture this?

12. *Have I shared my poem with another person?* The poem needs to speak independently. A poem that needs an explanation is like a joke that needs footnotes—it's not working. If I have to go beyond explaining the inspiration of the poem to saying, What I meant here was, then the poem needs rehabilitation; it can't walk without crutches.

Math and Poetry

Birds of a Feather

January 22 in Cleveland, the temperature in single digits and me out walking, balancing my sanity and dedication to a healthy heart against the wind chill factor. About two blocks out, my body temperature had risen to a point at which I could safely dislodge my chin from my collarbone and look around. Overhead I noticed a large V of geese heading (gasp) north.

North?

I wanted to jump up and down, wave my arms like a rescue victim, and scream, "Turn back while there's still time." It was still very much winter, shorts and sleeveless shirts at the mall notwithstanding. Had they fallen victim to some department store's jump-start advertising? To an offer for free airfare to a resort in Canada in the off season? Or was the leader, pumping madly and honking out directions to a flock of dedicated followers, researching the early-bird theory of worm accruement? I snugged my scarf a little tighter about my gaping mouth, frozen (almost) in time.

As they winged their way toward the cold stare of Lake Erie, I realized I didn't know enough about the habits of Canadian geese to suggest that these birdbrains were off track traveling north in January, but in terms of my birds-fly-south-in-the-fall-north-in-the-spring thinking, this sighting broke a pattern—thereby capturing my attention. It just didn't add up.

Oh, I know. The prerequisites of becoming a poet include walking around with one's head in the clouds and a singular detachment from the realities of living. It probably also helps to be missing a math gene. But although I do not balance my checkbook with any regularity, I am capable of simple addition. Granted, I never would have passed algebra/trig if Howie Fruman and Sammy Reese hadn't cheated me through it, but I know "doesn't add up" when I see it. And further, I happen to believe that mathematicians and poets have more in common than either group might believe.

Deeply ingrained in our thinking, much like the north/south, spring/fall pattern of bird migration, is the image of poets and mathematicians at odds with one another. Big odds. Think lions and gladiators. I can't be the only poet who began her college career by opening the undergraduate catalog and choosing a major that did not necessitate a single math course. I suspect many math majors (the future math teachers of the world) took exactly the opposite approach—choosing a major that did not have a poetry requisite. Am I right?

So, what could mathematicians and poets possibly have in common?

We look for patterns in the world. We attempt to find a pattern that we can apply in order to define the unknown. We both first look at nature as a whole and then attempt to break it down into parts. We use symbols to represent the unknown while we are in the process of defining terms, and we use comparative techniques to communicate with one another.

Even though I know these corollaries exist, it was with trepidation that I went on the Internet to search for the national math standards. What if they were in a language I couldn't translate? What if I couldn't find x (I've never had much luck with that elusive letter)? What if I just didn't get it? I typed "math" and "standards" into the search engine and had the mad but urgent instinct to fasten my seat belt like a space cadet heading into the great unknown.

But guess what? Math standards turned out to be the most organized and accessible of any in the content areas. Math folks have this logic and organization thing down. The standards are specific and clearly delineated by age group, and I could readily see exercises that would help support students who were striving to attain them. But I had to collect some samples from real kids, and I couldn't write with them in a language arts setting, as I usually do. I was going to have to venture into one of those classrooms I have structured my life to avoid. Math class.

Collecting student samples was an intimidating adventure. I was afraid even average twelve-year-olds would recognize immediately that I knew less about math than they did. Luckily, my daughter introduced me to a patient and enthusiastic math teacher, Mark Kevesdy, whose classroom is right down the hall from hers; he covered for me. Some of your students will be older, younger, more or less skilled than his students, but the samples are a benchmark (math lingo) for measuring student progress.

Mark dove in as we worked through the exercises, writing along with the kids. He even let us use him as a subject for a class writing activity. He told me he is accustomed to having the kids write in class, but usually in prose, to sum up a lesson. He doesn't even call his class "mathematics"—he calls it "think-a-matics"—and concentrates on putting math into real situations. Writing poetry in his class was a new adventure for both of us. The kids just thought it was cool.

Here's hoping your students do too.

Putting Shapes into Words: Building Concrete Poems

The study of math involves precise definitions and some very peculiar terms. *Congruent, polygon,* and *hypotenuse* are exacting words that are undoubtedly equal to the sum of their parts but they also read like a foreign language to many of us. Since poets are also into precise descriptions of images (and many of us are deemed to be peculiar), this would seem a natural place to begin to build a bridge between math and poetry. Having an image handy to help define such words can help with both comprehension and retention. Simple line drawings are one approach, but the "word drawing" of a *concrete poem* is another. A concrete poem consists of words cast in the shape of a poem's subject—a valentine poem shaped like a heart, a Halloween poem shaped like a pumpkin, a plank with wheels extolling the pleasures of skateboarding, or this poem in the shape of a balsam fir.

A
star
lights
ornaments
Christmas tree

Geometry Standard

Helps students use *visualization and spatial reasoning* while *building and drawing* geometric objects with specific *properties* and *recognize and apply geometric ideas and relationships in areas outside the mathematics classroom, such as art, science, and everyday life.*

◆ Build concrete poems about common shapes in and around the classroom.

◆ Begin by making a list of words and phrases that describe a common object, such as a snowman. (Okay, not so common in Arizona. Substitute a cactus.)

◆ Then arrange these terms so that they suggest the object's shape.

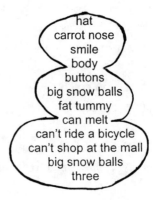

hat
carrot nose
smile
body
buttons
big snow balls
fat tummy
can melt
can't ride a bicycle
can't shop at the mall
big snow balls
three

◆ Challenge the students to take it to the next step—trapezoids (or hexagrams, or circles, or whatever). It's like picking up the object and holding it in one's hands, making the unfamiliar familiar.

◆ Start by composing a list of related words and phrases: four-sided, straight lines, and so on.

◆ Have students arrange the terms so that they suggest the shape.

◆ Decorate the room with these concrete poems as graphic reinforcements of the names and characteristics of these shapes.

◆ Assess students' comprehension of the shape being described and their ability to put the descriptors into the shape of the object.

FIG. 3–1 *Concrete Trapezoid Poem*

Create Math Poems That Utilize Patterns

Mathematics and poetry are all about patterns. The first patterns kids study in math are simple number sequences, and as we all know, these sequences become more and more complex and appear to be infinitely testable. Concurrently, kids often first learn about poetry through simple patterned verse. Recognizing patterns in writing helps students see mathematical patterns. Algebraically speaking, this will later help students with mathematical predictions.

The Limerick

Limericks are fun and a natural study in patterns. Mark's students had more trouble with the limerick pattern than either of us predicted. Depending on your students' skill, you may want to ask them to work in pairs. Here's a model limerick using an elementary math term.

There once was a student named Vlad
Who just couldn't learn how to add.
His face would turn red
As he scratched at his head
With doodles all over his pad.

◆ Share models of limericks aloud and/or on an overhead.

◆ Adapt the exercise to your course of study: *There once was a ruler named Straightedge . . .* or *There once was a blockhead named Cube . . .* (you get the picture).

◆ Let students share their limericks with one another, either aloud or by posting them around the room.

◆ Assess students' understanding of the math terminology, their ability to use the words in context, and their ability to follow a pattern. Mark asked his students to state the connection between math and this exercise. Here are some of their responses:

Like math, these poems have patterns and rules you have to follow.

We had to think about different meanings of some of the math terms (circle can be a noun or a verb for instance).

You can have fun with this, it's like a puzzle.

There once was a kid with malaria
He got from trying to get an area.
He would think and think
Trying to find the link.
When he finally got it he screamed in hysteria.
— Nicholas

There once was a kid next to me
Who couldn't learn Geometry.
He would always forget.
To learn every bit.
And his teacher would give him a D.
— Christa

The Slightly Abridged Sestina

This is a mathematical poetic form if there ever was one. It's all about numbers, thirty-nine lines in a predictable pattern. Unlike the limerick, this poem does not rhyme; its pattern is complex enough on its own. Because this pattern could challenge an experienced poet for weeks, the pattern has been abridged here to twenty-one lines (three six-line stanzas instead of six) to fit within an average class period. I suggest that you have students puzzle this out in pairs. In Mark's class, we were barely able to cram this lesson into a sixty-minute class period; you may want to take two class periods for this one, particularly if you have forty- or fifty-minute periods.

♦ Share my geometry abridged sestina on an overhead or the board and ask the students if they see a pattern. Can they translate the pattern into a number or letter sequence? *Hint:* The pattern is in the last word of each line (not necessarily the last word in a sentence). Solving this pattern sequence may take a while, so don't be too quick to give students the

> ### Geometry Standard
>
> Helps students *create and describe mental images of objects, patterns, and paths* while using a word *pattern* and *apply geometric ideas and relationships in areas outside the mathematics classroom, such as art, science, and everyday life.*
>
> Using this exercise with measurement terms or tools would of course reinforce a different set of math standards.

answer. This will build some momentum for writing their own abridged sestina. (I've taken the liberty of using plural versions of words, and your students may wish to do likewise. The point is to get them to use math terms correctly in patterned writing.)

♦ Have student pairs compose a list of six related math terms (e.g., measurement terms, arithmetic terms, geometry terms, etc.).

♦ Assign a number to each term, 1 to 6. One of these words will end each line of the poem. For example:

1. line

2. circle

3. square

4. rectangle

5. point

6. triangle

♦ Put the pattern of the sestina (see box) on the board or an overhead for easy reference. Depending on your students' ability and skill, you may use the abridged format or go for the whole sestina tamale, a multiclass-period word feast.

♦ Have student partners create their own poems using their six words in the prescribed pattern. Remind them that this is free verse, a little story with the words arranged in a pattern. Even though they have seen the pattern and read the model poem, you will probably have to reemphasize that the pattern is in the *line breaks,* which don't necessarily have to coincide with *sentence breaks.*

♦ Have students share their poems. Because of their intricate nature, it may be best to post the poems in addition to reading them aloud. Student pairs may exchange poems with each other to check that the pattern was followed, thereby reinforcing the learning.

◆ Assess students' ability to follow a prescribed pattern and use math terms correctly. These factors are more important than content. If Mark's students are a representative sampling, prepare yourself for science fiction.

Einstein was sitting at the center.
The field he was sitting in was shaped like a triangle.
He looked up at the sun at an odd angle.
Einstein found that the sun resembled a circle.
The sun was not a square, what a difference!
Then Einstein thought to himself, "The world is very
    wide."

Yes, the world is very wide.
Einstein was at the center
of his best thought, he picked up a snack shaped like
    a triangle.
"Food for thought," he said. "This pizza snack has a
    thirty-five-degree angle."
He scratched his head and walked in a small circle.
He looked at the time and noticed the difference.

There was a huge difference
between now and when he arrived. He spread his
    legs wide
and ran toward his home, in the center
of Bay Village. He looked in his window, shaped like
    a triangle.
What he saw surprised him. He ran through the
    door at an angle.
His son had drawn on the wall; there was a big circle.

"You've solved it," Einstein exclaimed. "A triangle's different
from a circle, angles
don't exist in circles. Your circle has such a wide center."

—Emily and Audrey, Grade 6

My dog's name is Euclid, he bolts out the
    door in a line.
Free at last, he circles
The front yard, stands on all fours and squares
Himself before racing in rectangles
From this point to that point.
He looks at me over his shoulder and
    triangles

Across the street. I follow the base of his
    triangle
As he turns next door and back. I'm tracing
    his line,
Holding his leash in a loopy circle.
I stop. He stops. We look each other square
In the eyes. I dare him to step out of that
    rectangle
of lawn. I look at my feet and point.

Come here! Of course he fails to see my point.
Bouncing up and down and sideways, he
    makes triangles
In the air. He sticks out his tongue, his tail a
    wavy line
As he barks, his mouth a perfect woof-woof
    circle.
He doesn't care. I swear, if he moves one
    more square
foot, he's angling his way into his rectangle

Of a cage for a year (or more). I circle point
once again. Put your rectangle square
at my feet, Euclid. Quit this racing in triangle
    lines!

—SARA HOLBROOK

Haiku: An ancient Japanese poetic pattern of three lines, each with a specified number of syllables:

> five syllables
> seven syllables
> five syllables

Haiku: False or True?

Poetry as a team sport? Why not. Back in Nero's time, poetry was an Olympic event. Even though he rigged the contest so that he was sure to win, you can most assuredly put together a fun and fair poetry-learning game in your classroom using haiku.

Haiku was once dedicated exclusively to the contemplation of nature. Today, much as we have Americanized Asian foods to fit our melting-pot tastes, we have modified this proud form of poetry to suit a broader range of topics than bubbling streams and mountain peaks. The format (see box) of the poem is exquisite in its simplicity.

Your students probably have encountered this poetic form in language arts, but they aren't putting pen to paper to reinforce that learning. They have math lessons to learn. Haiku is a great format for describing and defining terms and concepts. The compact pattern of the poem forces the poet to prioritize ideas.

◆ Brainstorm a list of math terms pertinent to the current unit of study—measurement terms, geometric terms, words relating to weight and volume, and so on.

◆ Divide the class into three or four teams and ask them to write haiku that define some of the words in *true* or *false* terms. Each team is to write one or more definition haiku, either accurate or purposefully inaccurate.

◆ After each team has written at least as many haiku as there are team members, have the teams play "stump the opposing team"—are the definitions true or false?

◆ Assess students' knowledge of the math terms being defined and their ability to follow a pattern.

Think you don't have time for this? The samples that follow were composed in exactly twenty-seven minutes, after which I went back and corrected one plural subject/singular verb.

Tangents break patterns
alone, making good time in
the wrong direction.

Parallelogram,
rectangle lines short and long
with a sideways slant.

Circle swirls around
in diameter belt, can't
put its points in line.

Three points, three straight lines,
three right angles, and a base:
voila! Triangle.

Zero! You're nothing!
Can't add, divide, multiply.
Can't even subtract.
Just the middle man:
positive and negative—
you stuck in between.

If you've been thinking that writing poetry is an otherworldly pursuit, one that could never work in a busy math classroom, put that idea in the wastebasket beside your desk. It's weighing you (and your students) down. Think of writing poems like these as a trip to the driving range—quantity is your clearest shot at quality. One of the reasons I was able to write six haiku in less than a half hour is that I have written hundreds of poems; I'm practiced. I practiced for years, unself-consciously, at the kitchen table, next to a flat Diet Coke, with the family tornado swirling around me, and the clock on the stove counting down some soccer/play/dance practice or airplane departure deadline. Neither total silence nor total isolation is needed for all writing. Giving students time to practice their writing freely and unself-consciously is not just fun, it is one of the most useful learning situations you can provide in your classroom.

Your students will create better ones, and they'll do it within the class period. Here are two by a trio of students in Mark's class.

> It uses four lines.
> Parallel pairs make a square,
> angles at ninety.
>
> The area is
> the space inside of a shape:
> multiply the sides.
>
> —Christa, Elizabeth,
> and Tori, Grade 6

Writing haiku is not quantitative analysis; it is quick and easy. But it is also an effective way for students to put their knowledge to work and to practice their writing skills at the same time.

Family Poems: Bringing It All Back Home

Whenever and wherever I look in the mathematics standards, the word *relationship* keeps popping up. Finding and describing relationships seems to be a core component of mathematical communication, as it is of poetical communication. As poets we are always looking at and for relationships to delicately define our terms so that we may occasionally hook our readers, slick as a tender top-water, small-mouth bass fisherman. According to the *Principles and Standards of School Mathematics*, "college-level mathematics courses are increasingly emphasizing the ability to convey ideas clearly, both orally and in writing. To be prepared for the future, students must be able to exchange mathematical ideas effectively with others." As a poet, I know that one of the most direct ways to construct effective communication is by referencing relationships—*I saw what I saw and it looked like this*. Using a poet's sensibilities to create mathematical communications, finding and describing how things relate to one another using precise language, can only help us to meet standards goals in math.

At Home Arithmetically

In this poem, I use arithmetic terms to describe one of the most basic and fundamental of all relationships—the family. In my case, my children grew up with two houses to live in, thereby increasing the number of names on their contact-in-an-emergency cards at school and decreasing the probability that their soccer shoes would be at the right house on game day. We can all laugh about this now that they are grown, but at the time none of us thought there was one single positive in the divorce equation. In fact, it wasn't until I wrote this poem, making a thoughtful extra effort to include the word *multiply,* that I began to see a good side to the issue. Divorce had enabled us to multiply our parts; it had not only taken away from but also added to our lives.

◆ Brainstorm a list of arithmetic terms. (Details like this are the stuff of poetry. Gather lots of details, the more precise the better.) They might include some of the following terms or focus specifically on measurement terms if that is the subject of your classroom study:

> quantity
> order/sequence
> great—small
> unit
> attributes
> primary
> measurement
> size
> weight

◆ Ask students to work from this list, picking and choosing the terms they think might apply to their family.

◆ If some of the terms require research, that might become a homework assignment. (The collective weight of the family, for instance, could turn into a poem incorporating fractions.)

Divided

We're not a unit
    anymore.
The family got divided.
When birthdays come,
I get two cakes,
But don't get too excited.

Two birthdays
Can be kind of sad.

I'm learning to
Subtract and add
Faces to my party list.
Some are great,
And others missed.

Birthdays didn't stop
    because
Divorce divided up our
    hearts.
Now we party separately,
But get to multiply the
    parts.

—SARA HOLBROOK,
I Never Said I Wasn't Difficult

- Ask the students to turn their lists into a poem. If they want to work in a pattern, that's cool (see page 17 on quatrains). Free verse works just as well.

- Since one of our goals is to communicate mathematical ideas to peers, when the poems are finished, build in time for sharing aloud. Start by having students share in pairs, then in small groups, and finally with the class as a whole.

- Assess whether the writer is able to make others understand the dimensions of their family using mathematical terms.

Family Poems: At Home Geometrically

Still working with my own divided/multiplied family (poetry is very personal that way), I decided to take a crack at a new concept. To look at the family in geometric terms—looking at us as a family-of-four square that split diagonally into two triangles, turning us from a four-sided figure to two three-sided figures. (That was before there were step-siblings and step-gerbils involved, which would require math skills in multidimensional shapes that I can't even name.)

Weird Math, or How
2 + 2 − 1 = 6

Two parents + two kids
Equals family of four.
It's square, but it's stable
Till one parent splits and

Diagonally-walks out the door.
When parents triangulate,
Kids can't stop the dissection,
Instead they are pulled
By opposing points
In two different directions.

—Sara Holbrook

- Brainstorm a list of geometric terms and shapes.

- Have each student choose a geometric shape that fits her or his family.

- Have students fold a piece of paper in half lengthwise.

- On one half of the paper, ask them to list the characteristics of the geometric figure they chose.

- On the other half of the paper, ask them to list the characteristics of their families that led them to chose this figure.

- Ask students to create a poem from their lists and then illustrate the poem by incorporating the figure within or beside or surrounding the poem.

- Have students share the resulting poems by posting them on the wall, with illustrations (perhaps computer-generated), and/or reading them aloud.

- Assess students' understanding of their chosen geometric shape and their ability to build an argument that relates their family to that shape.

Over the Top: Measurements Poems

> ### Measurement Standard
>
> Helps students *understand measurable attributes of objects and the units, systems, and processes of measurement,* thus causing them to *apply appropriate techniques, tools, and formulas to determine measurements.*

"*Mathematics* is a verb, not just a noun," says Sherman K. Stein, professor of mathematics at the University of California. He points out that in reading mathematics, nothing can be skipped. In other words, we can't skim the math chapter as we might an article on the sports page, skipping the words we don't know, attempting to absorb the general meaning. While it is the responsibility of the author to make mathematical arguments clear, it is the responsibility of the reader to play an active role in understanding the text by reading carefully and knowing the meaning of every term. "Oh, close enough," is not the phraseology of brain surgery or math—both require precision. Mathematics "must be read word by word, symbol by symbol." The math teacher, then, has to be concerned with student comprehension of vocabulary.

The measurement standards are broken down into two main categories: understanding units and systems of measurement and choosing the right tools and formulas to determine measurements. Seems simple enough—as long as students are familiar with the terms and the language of measurement. The following exercises are designed to help students practice using math terminology to further their comprehension and to help teachers assess their capabilities—and hopefully to have a little fun in the process.

Greater Than/Less Than

I could improve my Scrabble game in a major way if I could manage to memorize all those weird little words incorporating *j, x,* or *z.* And I've tried, I've really tried. But since I have very little call to use words like *azo* in my life, they evaporate quicker than cheap cologne. We need to put new terms into practice for them to stick. I'm going to make a quantum leap here and speculate that this is also true when it comes to math symbols. In this exercise, students incorporate math symbols in a poem describing themselves.

◆ Have students divide a piece of paper in half lengthwise, making two columns.

◆ In one column, have them list things they are greater than, in the other column, things they are less than. Encourage precision and humor. They are trying to reinforce the learning of greater than/less than by putting themselves in the picture.

Greater Than	Less Than
a sparrow	an elephant
my toothbrush	the gymnasium
this stapler	a tank

◆ Next, have them substitute symbols for the words *greater than/less than* to create a list poem.

> I'm > a sparrow, but < an elephant.
> I'm > my toothbrush, but < the gym.
> I'm > this stapler, but < a tank.

◆ Have students share their poems with one another.

◆ Ask students to save the poems in their math notebooks or journals. As new symbols are learned (equal to, not equal to, etc.), have the students add to the poem throughout the year. It's fun to get ridiculous with these, as long as it can be determined that the student actually comprehends the symbol.

◆ Assess by having students trade papers. If the reader disagrees with the author, the author should be able to provide an argument to support her theory of greater than/less than.

The Benchmark Is Me!

At Center Street Elementary School in Mentor, Ohio, the fifth grade was studying measurement. Included in this unit are the symbols for (and concepts of) greater than and less than, along with a new word: *benchmark*. If we assume that at the beginning of the school year, head still full of chlorine from the city pool, the average fifth grader understands a *benchmark* to be the creases left on the back of her legs after sitting too long on the bleachers, writing a poem using *benchmark* helps unlock the mystery of its mathematical meaning.

And what better way to unlock a mystery than to create a riddle? Using the greater than/less than model and a common tag line, Frankie (age eleven) created this riddle poem:

> > an eraser but < an elephant
> > an atom but < a house
> > a pencil but < a cow
> < a blue whale > a mouse
>
> Can't you see?
> The benchmark is me!

After creating poems using the new word and listening to classmates' poems, it's doubtful any student will ever forget what *benchmark* means.

- Have students write their poems using themselves as the benchmarks.

- Have students share their poems aloud in small groups and then with the class as a whole.

- Try this exercise with other math vocabulary words. Students can have fun making up poems to go with the following taglines:

> The *remainder* is me!
> The *sum* is me!

- Assess students' ability to follow the pattern of the poem incorporating and showing an understanding of the symbols and the meaning of a mathematical term.

Benchmark II: The Sequel

Now that you have the basics, get a little creative with your riddles.

- Change the benchmark from a fifth grader to, say, that colossal pine tree on the corner. How does that change the content of the poem? (Okay, I picked *tree* because it rhymes with *see*. You or your students can come up with something even better—and more measurable.)

> > a pine cone < a redwood
> > a squirrel < a mountain
> > a candy bar < the ocean
> Can't you see?
> The benchmark is a pine tree!

Problem-Solving Standard

Enables students to *build new mathematical knowledge through solving problems that arise in mathematics and other contexts* and *to apply and to adapt a variety of appropriate strategies to solve problems as they monitor and reflect on the process of mathematical problem solving.*

Benchmark III: The Saga Continues

◆ What if you look at greater than/less than comparisons in terms of circumference? length? speed? Every time you change the criteria or the *benchmark*, you create a new poem.

◆ As you move through the unit on measurement, ask students to create a riddle poem for each new term they encounter and staple them together in a book called *My Measurement Poems*, creating a keepsake reminder of new terms.

Benchmark IV: Variables?

You mean the answers to these problems aren't cast in stone? I thought there was always a right and a wrong in math. Are you telling me we can change the rules when the problem is in the air?

Okay. This is personal. My approach to variables is the result of a grudge match I had with Miss London in junior high. It was one of the most difficult lessons for me to learn in math and is perhaps a *benchmark* in my decline in the field.

To a kid (me, for instance) raised on fact sheets and dittos, the whole concept of problems with variables didn't fit. Remember those endless sheets of problems with the purple print that smelled funny and smeared under sweaty hands? I liked those. They were quick homework, good for a check in the grade book, and you could watch *Disney* on Sunday nights and do them at the same time. I was a star at worksheets. Sometimes the teacher would even let me use the key and correct those of other kids. Or we would trade the worksheets and she'd put the answers on the board. The important thing about math was, the answer was either right or wrong.

So when I hit the middle grades and poor Miss London, with her wide turquoise eyes, tried to introduce the concept of variables to me in terms of letter symbols, I protested. *What do you mean, if we add* a *to* x, *what happens to* y*? Who knows? What am I, a mind reader? Who cares about* x*? Put him back in the drawer.*

I like the letter a *better, anyway. It's bigger than* y, *case closed. Variables? What is this, a joke?*

◆ Go back to the greater than/less than poems and ask students to add a *variable* they can picture, an image that will help them visualize the mathematical concept. Adding variables to poems makes for some fun creative writing while reinforcing a basic math concept and visualizing problem solving.

◆ Ask the students under what circumstances a kid could be bigger than a colossal pine tree. What kind of variable would make this equation true? In other language: me + x > colossal pine tree. (Possible answers might include a chain saw, stilts, a jet pack, or climbing the ladder limbs of the pine tree up to the top and shoving a fist in the air above its spire.)

◆ Have the students choose one greater than/less than line out of their poems and rewrite, incorporating a variable. Can a person be greater than a pine tree but less than a pencil? What variables might make that possible?

◆ Assess the students' understanding of the meaning and use of the word *variable*.

100 Percent Poetry: It All Adds Up

This one is fun. It evolved from a real-life experience. I once described myself to a very competent and patient therapist as 30 percent executive, 30 percent mom, 30 percent poet, and 10 percent yuppie. At the time, I was seeking professional help to suppress my poet (read *nonsense*) percentage in a personal effort to *get back to basics*. As the kind doctor pointed out to me, success in life (in or out of math class) is based on the ability to accept all the parts that add up to the whole.

Depending on the skill of your students, these percentages can be approximate—or for real. For instance (see sidebar on page 77), I have absolutely no idea if I am precisely ".6%" eye-

Number and Operations Standard

Helps students *compute fluently and make reasonable estimates;* develop *fluency in adding, subtracting, multiplying, and dividing whole numbers;* use *fractions and decimals in situations relevant to students' experience;* use *a visual model;* and *add and subtract commonly used fractions and decimals.* Causes students to develop and use strategies to estimate the results of rational-number computations, estimate equivalent ratios, and judge the reasonableness of the results.

brows. I'm not sure I could figure that out even with all the right measuring tools. However, that doesn't mean I can't still have fun with the concept of percentages. When the "whole" is not merely a number, but is "me," the situation is (as math standards suggest) "relevant to the students' experience."

Listed among the standards for all grade levels is a directive that students should be able to judge the "reasonableness" of estimations of parts of a whole. Acknowledging certain variables, under what *reasonable* circumstance might we describe a teacher as *80 percent eyebrows, 5 percent tapping foot, 5 percent frown, and 10 percent folded arms?* a student missing homework? late to class?

Writing poems incorporating percentages helps kids understand and visualize the concept of wholes and fractions and incorporate (comfortably) that kind of math talk into their writing. (This is a good activity at the beginning of the year, when you

100% Me

10% giggles
10% tears
12% confidence
8% fears
2% pizza
3% sighs
30% homework
5% lies
9% messy
6% neat
0.6% eyebrows
4.4% feet

It all adds up, can't you
    see:
The total is 100% me!

—SARA HOLBROOK

FIG. 3–2 *Mark's 100% Me Poem*

are getting to know students. It lets you see how they perceive themselves. Katie has also used this exercise with students to build characterizations in their study of how S. E. Hinton describes the characters in the first two chapters of *The Outsiders*. In her words, "Characterization. They get it now!")

◆ Read "100% Me" to the students as a model.

◆ Develop a "100% Me" poem as a group. (In Mark's class, we used him—aka Mr. K—as our subject, which worked great. See page 77.) Spend about five minutes listing characteristics of the subject on the board. These might include physical characteristics, interests, skills, and so on. Some of Mr. K's characteristics were:

> smart
> math
> dad
> Ohio State University
> koosh ball [he tosses one of these around the classroom during question-and-answer sessions]
> think-a-matics
> eyebrows
> feet
> bald spot [ouch]
> Einstein's fan
> coach
> enthusiastic

◆ Next, assign percentages to the characteristics. This may involve a great deal of discussion but should only take about ten minutes. Students should be prepared to defend the reasonableness of their estimations. (For instance, I think it is fair to say that Mr. K's feet are bigger than his eyebrows—thank goodness!)

◆ Have students make a list of their own characteristics. Do they have curls? like to read? have a favorite food, team, color, pet, music group, movie?

- Have students assign percentages to their characteristics. Depending on their skills, you might want to ask that one or two of the percentages be based on a precise measurement in order to assess the students' abilities to calculate percentages. (Don't require that *all* the percentages be precisely accurate: That will remove all the weird pizza from the poems.)

- Ask students to turn this into a poem. Can they think of an interesting lead-in or conclusion that makes this poem uniquely theirs? It's not necessary to include all the listed characteristics; they will have to do some prioritizing.

- Have students illustrate these poems with a pie chart, graph, or whatever fits into the lesson.

- Assess students' comprehension of percentages, adding decimals, and summarizing the whole and its parts. A student whose total adds up to 475 percent clearly needs some coaching before test time rolls around.

All the authors of the poems that follow are sixth graders in Mark's class. (Their poems were so adorable, it was difficult to chose just a few.)

100% Ryan

I am 30% plump
3% brown hair
10% Mr. Peanut Worship
20% football
10% red
2% braces
5% marshmallows
And I'm 20% jolly
If you add it all up
It is equivalent to me.
   —Ryan, Grade 6

100% Me

10% horses
8% pizza
4% sandy brown hair
12% shopping
10% dogs
2% orange
1% quiet
15% Sims
16% AOL
12% fun
and 10% school
If you add it all up
you will see,
all those together
equal 100% me.
   —Natalie, Grade 6

I'm Very Rare

I'm 9% math
10% soccer
4% science
2% clean locker
I'm 21% wilderness
6% blue
I'm 6% braces
and 2% shoe
I'm 33% smiles
3% brown hair
4% pineapple
I'm very rare!
   —Kelsey, Grade 6

Number and Operations Standard

Helps students increase their *understanding of numbers, ways of representing numbers,* and *relationships among numbers and number systems; understand the place-value structure of the base-ten number system; be able to represent and compare whole numbers and decimals and describe their characteristics and the nature of their factors;* and *develop meaning for integers and represent and compare quantities with them.*

It Figures: A Visit to the Number Doctor

In Aimee Bender's novel, *An Invisible Sign of My Own,* a kind of grown-up version of Jon Sciescka's *Math Curse,* the narrator is an oh-so-slightly obsessive/compulsive young woman who describes herself as a quitter of everything in her life except her fascination with numbers.

> After all that, the one thing I loved but never quit, could not seem to give up, was, of all things, math. I tried to stop thinking about numbers but found myself, against my will, adding my steps and multiplying the people in the park against one another, knocking on wood in careful rhythm, counting endlessly: sheep, students, parents, age, heartbeats. Mix up some numbers and signs, and you get an equation for the way the wind shifts or an axiom for the movement of water, or the height of someone, or for how skin feels. You can account for softness. You can explain everything. Even air is just an arrangement of digits, and with just the right balance—poof! We breathe.
>
> I've spent entire afternoons thinking about one number, flying down its long onyx tunnel, opening up the trap door that it is. Take 5. Seems regular—five-dollar bill, five-minute break—but five is also the sum of two squares, and a prime, and pentagrams, and my sixth-grade math teacher told me that the Pythagoreans thought 5 was about marriage because it was 3 (their first odd) joined with a 2 (their first even). . . .
>
> I heard about a woman who got a job reordering an entire town. The numbers were off because the mayor had a counting problem, and she'd been hired to come in and reintroduce 8. It's been missing in some clocks. She'd also needed to go over the books and see if the adding was correct (which of course it wasn't, without 8) and to check all the signs. Drivers were apparently getting off the highway, following the sign that said Gas: 2 miles, to find nothing but dusty roads. The sign was supposed to say 28. It was a whole industry, townsfolk dashing over to gasless cars with cans of portable petrol. She was called a number doctor. That was my dream job.

Unfortunately for the protagonist (but fortunately for the reader—this book is poignant/hilarious/fascinating), she does not get her dream job. Instead, she is drafted into a position as a math teacher at the local school, where when she arrives:

I was very disappointed to see that the math classroom had no windows and was the width of a hallway. Also it smelled like concrete. *Art* and *spelling* were squarer, and windowed, and scented with sunshine, so I figured math gets the shaft in classroom selection because the math teacher is the dentist of the school curriculum. . . .

The math teacher as dentist. Both misunderstood and stereotyped and trying to work pain free! Imagine yourself asking the class to open wide. When they all comply, as students naturally do, try feeding them this writing exercise to help deepen their understanding of individual numbers.

In this tanka, I've incorporated some of Bender's descriptors of the number 5. I realize that this and other rigid poetic forms may seem foreign (and not just in a geographic sense) in the math classroom, but because they are produced using set patterns, in many ways they fit better there than in a traditional language arts classroom. Typically, the tanka deals with nature or a season of the year, but here is used it to describe one of the most basic elements of nature—a single number.

> **Tanka:** A Japanese poetic pattern of five lines, each with a specified number of syllables.
>
> > five syllables
> > seven syllables
> > five syllables
> > seven syllables
> > seven syllables

> Five's a prime number.
> Regularly, it adds up:
> two squared plus one squared.
> Five sums up a pentagram,
> then takes a five-minute break.

◆ Share the model tanka with students, perhaps on an overhead. Count the syllables. Ask the students if the facts are correct.

◆ Write the formula for the tanka pattern on the board.

◆ Have the students, individually or in pairs, identify a number for their own tanka poem. Depending on their skill, numbers could range from 0 to 23,678,495, and beyond.

◆ Ask students to research facts about that number.

◆ Have students compose their own tanka. These are fun to illustrate and post.

◆ Assess students' ability to follow the pattern and to correctly describe their chosen number.

> Odd numbers are cool
> Odd, opposite of even
> Two odds get even
> Half of the numbers are odd
> I hope you like odds like me!
> —Matt and Nick, Grade 6

If I Were a Zero

Symbolic representations in thinking and writing are an inherent component of both mathematical and poetical logic. This exercise gives legs to an inanimate object and is so old and so well used by so many poets, I can't figure out on whom to bestow the original credit. My poem in the box, modeled after many before me, was written for adults, but I use it regularly with middle-grade students. If they ask me about the word *desire,* I explain it's like a plate of cookies on top of the fridge, out of reach. If you'd rather not go down that path with your fourth graders (and I'm not recommending that you do), just use the first and last stanzas as a pattern model. The pattern, repeating the *if I were a* line at the beginning and end of each stanza, is still easily grasped.

◆ Show as much of the poem as works with your students on an overhead, or read it aloud.

◆ Depending on what you're studying in math at the time, have students choose a related term to incorporate into the poem. A brainstormed list might include:

> a zero
> an equivalent
> a compass
> a cube

a whole number

a decimal point

♦ Have students use the term to write their own *if I were* poems.

♦ Let students perform their poems aloud, or post them (along with illustrations) in your classroom or even outside in the hall.

♦ Assess the veracity of students' poems.

It's a Paradox!

When I was cruising through the math standards and zoomed by the observation that students need to "sharpen and extend their reasoning skills by deepening their evaluations of their assertions and conjectures by using inductive and deductive reasoning," I screeched to a halt. Reasoning belongs to math? Cool! Talk about a skill that needs to be taught across the curriculum! The next generation very much needs to be able to make some good, sensible decisions about the world, which, let's face it, preceding generations have left in a bit of a mess.

The standards caution that many students begin third grade "believing that something is true because it has occurred before, because they have seen several examples of it, or because their experience to date seems to confirm it." Indeed, I'm sure they do. But I wouldn't confine that to kids in the third through fifth grades. *My car always started when I turned the key before....* We all fall victim to this kind of loose logic. One of the reasons for combining math

If I Were a Poem

If I were a poem
I would grab you by the ankles
and rustle you up to your every leaf.
I would gather your branches
in the power of my winds and pull you skyward,
if I were a poem.

If I were a poem
I would walk you down beside the rushing stream,
swollen with spring,
put thunder in your heart,
then lay you down, a new lamb,
to sing you to softly sleep,
if I were a poem.

If I were a poem,
I wouldn't just talk to you of
politics, society, and change,
I would be a raging bonfire
to strip you of your outer wrap
and then I would reach within
and with one touch
ignite the song in your own soul,
if I were a poem.

If I were a poem
I would hold my lips
one breath away from yours
and inflate you with such desire
as can exist only just out of reach,
and then I would move
the breadth of one bee closer,
not to sting,
but to brush you with my wings
as I retreat, to leave you holding
nothing but a hungry,
solitary sigh,
if I were a poem.

If I were a poem
my thoughts would finally be put to words
by your own poetry,
I would push you that far.
If I,
if I were a poem.

—SARA HOLBROOK,
Chicks Up Front

skills with writing skills is to bring reasoning skills out of math class and into real life.

One of the chasms between language arts and math and science is in how we treat the words *argument* and *persuasion*. In language arts class, students learn persuasion by picking a point of view (for or against the death penalty, abortion, equal rights) and then researching facts to support opinions. In math and science, they learn to use facts to form their opinions, a more reasonable concept to be sure.

According to the standards, "during [the middle] grades, formulating conjectures and assessing them on the basis of evidence should become the norm. Students should learn that several examples are not sufficient to establish the truth of a conjecture and that counterexamples can be used to disprove a conjecture. They should learn that by considering a range of examples, they can reason about the general properties and relationships they find." And further, "they should expand the audience for their mathematical arguments beyond their teacher and their classmates. They need to develop compelling arguments with enough evidence to convince someone who is not part of their own learning community."

Poetry can help with this challenge.

◆ Use the poem "Paradox" as a model to encourage students to exercise their math reasoning skills to create a similar poem.

◆ Brainstorm a list of topics that are known to have arguments for and against, positives and negatives, pluses and minuses. (A math professor friend of mine suggested I use *pluses* and *minuses* to describe these opposing characteristics because, in the strictest sense, every negative must have a corresponding positive. Mark's students seemed more comfortable with the words *positive* and *negative,* so we went with those. I'll leave it up to you.) Here's the list Mark's class came up with:

ice cream

taking out the trash

working for my dad

walking the dog

having a pet

money

sharing a room

scary movies

chores

homework

◆ Have students choose one of the preceding as a subject (or maybe they can think of a better one). The important thing is that the subject has more than one side to it.

◆ Have them fold a piece of paper in half and list the pluses and minuses of their chosen issue, looking for the one deal breaker. Take *ice cream* for instance:

Plus	**Minus**
yummy	fattening
cool on the throat	bad for your teeth
lots of flavors	
a good family destination on a hot summer night	

◆ Ask students to convert their lists into a "paradox" poem.

◆ Have the students read the poems aloud in small groups or to the group as a whole. Let the audience discuss the poems, how the truth about ice cream (or whatever) involves positives and negatives (pluses and minuses), and how we use this type of logic to make decisions and to develop arguments.

◆ Assess evidence that the student understands the concept of a paradox and is able to articulate it with figurative language.

Lauren presents a list of positives and one negative in her poem about sharing a room with her sister.

> Sharing a room
> is like sharing with a beast
> Everything's a mess
> I can't even get dressed
> Making so much noise
> I can't find my toys
> Taking all my stuff
> thinks that she's so tough
> She's crossed the line
>
> At least someone's on my side.

Thomas takes the opposite approach, listing all the positive thoughts about his allowance, bringing him to one negative: when he spends it all, he's broke.

> Getting your allowance
> now what to do
> the smell of it
> I know
> what
> to do
> I will spend
> it that's what
> I'll do. I'll spend
> it on toys, candy,
> food, shirts.
> Oh, no. Broke.

Other students, like Joey, mix it up.

> Eating some ice cream
> very cold on my teeth
> Even though it's fattening,
> it's really, really sweet.
> Cools me down when I'm hot
> but costs me some money

Yes, ice cream is creamy
and ice cream is yummy.
But something will happen
if you eat too much.

By doing a little cross-training in math and language arts, we can strengthen learning in both disciplines, not only to the benefit of the students, but also to the benefit of the schools and teachers as we work together to meet national, state, and local content-area standards. After you have brought a few of these exercises into your math classroom, you may wish to peruse the other connections in the remaining chapters.

4 ~ Science and Poetry

A Rose by Any Other Name . . .

Ever think you have an infallible hypothesis and then go looking for data to prove your contention? A contention that you were really, really sure was *absolutely* true? And then you found out that some of your assumptions were outdated and in fact really, really off base?

See, in undertaking this argument that poetry can be a practical vehicle for teaching across the content areas, I had this hypothesis that the science department would be the toughest sell. We live in a technologically demanding world that from where I sit is gaining on me hard and fast. Communication today is most often described in terms of speed and megabytes of volume rather than rhythm and metaphor. Tech folks (I assumed) must think that the art of poetry is best a trivial, quaint indulgence, certainly not a form of communication in an intergalactic sense. Right? I would support my hypothesis by defending the need for the exacting language of poetry in a scientific community traveling into the future at warp speed, proving that poets should be allowed into the science classroom since writing poetry engages kids in the high-level reasoning recommended by the *National Science Education Standards.* That was the hypothesis.

Writing poetry about science not only teaches language lessons but also reinforces content learning and sparks curiosity. If we write poems about migrating butterflies, haiku about snakes, or questioning poems about drug use, the facts we collect and use to do so are much less likely to flutter off, as they tend to do the day after the science test. Poetry is like aspirin in providing benefits that are sometimes difficult to explain, but we have data to prove that the benefits exist. Poetry works.

But when I started to dig around in the standards and on the National Science Teachers Association website, I discovered that language arts is much more on the minds of school science departments than I ever thought possible. It has to be. After all, standardized tests focus on reading comprehension and math skills for the most part, starving science departments and forcing teachers to look for ways to elbow the birds and the bees and the rocks and the trees into the language arts curriculum.

Sidelining poets is a sad state of affairs, but to tell you the truth, we're kind of used to it. It's a centuries-long tradition. As a child of the age of *Sputnik,* however, I never expected to be sharing a bench at the side of the education arena with the science department. Then came the No Child Left Behind Act, which states: "States must administer an annual assessment of student achievement in science at least once in grades 3–5, 6–9, and 10–12, beginning in 2007."

In 2007? It's okay that technological, environmental, and genetic studies (just to name a paltry few) *are* left behind until then? According to the *Illinois School Report Card 2003,* students in the third grade spend an average of 30 minutes a day on science education and 146 minutes a day on language arts. Things improve slightly by eighth grade, when kids are spending an average of 44 minutes a day on science, as opposed to 94 minutes on language arts. But of the four major content areas, time spent on science consistently comes in last.

Leave Behinds

Edison thought up the lightbulb,
records, and phonographs.
Curie perfected the X-ray;
Knute Rockne, the forward pass.

Salk made vaccinations,
Ford, the Model T,
Disney, Mickey Mouse,
and I—
watch my TV.

I'm nestled in this world
that bold inventors built.
Will my leave behinds
be just my junk food trash
and guilt?

What made two bicycle makers fly?
What made my couch potato state?
What if I turned off the tube
and let my leisure time create?

I wonder what I'd make.

—SARA HOLBROOK,
Nothing's the End of the World

What can I say? Welcome to my bench? Maybe as we sit here for a minute we can put our heads together and come up with some way to join forces? For instance, if we write *about* the birds and the bees and the rocks and the trees, aren't we advancing both kids' language skills and their knowledge about the science of our world? Makes sense to me. Sadly, however, what makes sense to too many districts is to cut science out of the curriculum entirely to raise the scores of students who are scrambling to meet high-stakes reading and writing goals.

I now realize that my suggestion that we squeeze poetry lessons into a crowded, endangered science curriculum may be more of an irritation to the science department than I ever imagined. Time, that ineluctable factor in all equations, is as we all know limited. How do we do such a thing in the precious twenty, thirty, or forty-five minutes a day devoted to our world?

My hypothesis changed. I needed to build a twofold argument that (1) writing poetry in science class can be a method of reinforcing content learning standards, and (2) science poetry can provide another way to meet the overwhelming demands of the high-stakes language arts tests.

I once did a writing workshop in a seventh-grade classroom in Florida, a stifling little portable, one among about forty in back of the school. As I approached the building, I asked the teacher, "What are these kids studying in science?" thinking that we could use that lesson as a basis for our writing. She replied, "Oh, these kids don't get science. They are not reading up to grade level, so they only get language arts and math because that's all that's on the test." Seeing my eyes widen into saucers, the teacher quickly apologized, "I know, it's ridiculous, but that's where we are," as she opened the door on one of the most miserable classrooms I have ever set foot in. I went back to the hotel room that night and cried. No science at all? No mapping trips across the Yukon or identifying naked mole rats to help engage these students in reading and learning? And this was being passed off as education? Who's kidding whom? I do not have national statistics on this, but unfortunately Florida is not the only state in which I have encountered kids being deprived of science lessons so that they can spend two, three, even four class periods a day reviewing for high-stakes language arts tests.

I hope that after reviewing these writing exercises you won't see poetry as an irritant, but more like the pink lotion that makes the itch go away. Why? Because communication can never really be measured only in terms of speed and volume. What we have to say will always be more important than how fast technology allows us to say it. No scientific discovery can advance the field unless the scientist is able to put it into words. Poetry is not some Stone Age relic to be analyzed, cataloged, and shelved for possible further study. It is a dynamic method of recording experience and making decisions.

The sheer amount of data in the knowledgeable world has led us to increasing specialization; no longer do we pretend there is no distinction between a scientist, poet, or philosopher as they did back in Ancient Greece (see next sidebar). Rarely do you find a person able to acknowledge that she is a poet–scientist. She had to declare a major early on and pursue one or the other. In fact, no one is even just a scientist anymore; one isn't even an anthropologist, astronomer, or biologist. Instead, one is a genetic epidemiologist, a pomologist, or (I love this one) an epidemiological pharmacoepigeneticist (eh?).

Some will say specialization is essential to advance the world technologically; others see such narrowing of focus as downright dangerous, with the specialities unable to relate to one another. Every time we turn on our computers or pop an antibiotic we are reminded of the benefits of specialization, but it is also important to remember what such compartmentalizing puts us in danger of losing—for example, our ability to look at the whole world working in concert. I presume that this is the rational behind that first standard and the reasons for the emphasis in the standards on the need for communication.

Poets, philosophers, and scientists have the potential to band together and give the world a more unified view and support our specialties as long as we can talk to one another. With a shared vision we can work together to help the world community by improving our powers of observation and then, as Salinger states, by acquiring a well-developed "ability to report back."

> I am enough of an artist to draw freely upon my imagination. Imagination is more important than knowledge. Knowledge is limited. Imagination encircles the world.
>
> —ALBERT EINSTEIN

Is there conclusive evidence that writing poetry in science class will meet all the goals listed in the *National Science Education Standards?* No. But along with microscopes, beakers, and teaspoons, poetry is another important tool in helping kids make the essential connections that will guide them on their path to learning.

Poetry's mission is to understand the universe—physics' mission is the same. Both condition the mind to search for answers, to stimulate imagination, to look beyond the status quo. The arts and sciences are intertwined more than either side seems to want to admit.

Astonishing elements of scientific theory can be found in poetry written decades and even hundreds of years before scientists proposed their existence. In fact in Ancient Greece there was no distinction between a scientist, poet, or philosopher. Back in 400 BCE Democritus (a philosopher-poet) postulated that the universe was composed of minute invisible entities, atoms. Thus the birth of atomic physics. Not the discovery of atoms but the concept of atoms. It is the philosopher-poet section of the brain that is responsible for imagining what the universe is. Then the pragmatic scientist part sets out to prove it.

A good piece of writing asks questions; a great piece proposes answers. It is this stepping out into the light with an idea that advances the pursuit of the truth. It is the equivalent of a hypothesis in science. But before this can take place one must have a well-developed imagination in order to come up with the notion in the first place.

Poetry exercises the mind to imagine, to think in metaphors, to make comparisons between things, to see beyond what is obvious. This strengthening of the creative portion of the mind can only enhance the pursuit of truth in any discipline, including science. Conversely, the objective nature of scientific proof can amplify the poet's imagination by giving him a base with which to start his search. Instead of reinventing the wheel, he starts inside the vehicle, already driving. Understanding the mechanics of a lightening storm in no way leaves it any less wonderful.

Newton said, "If I see far, it is because I stand on the shoulders of giants." It is this sentiment that personifies our search for the truth. There are a lot of giants out there; some are poets, and some are scientists, teachers, parents, and friends. Don't be afraid to climb on any of their shoulders and see what you can see; just be sure you have the ability to report back.

—MICHAEL SALINGER, AUTHOR OF
Neon: Poems and Stories.

The science content standards are divided into eight categories:

Unifying concepts and processes in science
A. Science as inquiry
B. Physical science
C. Life science
D. Earth and space science
E. Science and technology
F. Science in personal and social perspectives
G. History and nature of science

The exercises in this chapter are designed to be used in multiple categories. For example, if the topic of one writing exercise happens to be gravity, using the same exercise with a technology concept addresses a different standard. Look beyond the exercise specifics and you will see many different ways to apply the lessons and to adapt them to your unit of study.

"The cognitive sciences grew up studying cognition—rational thought," states cognitive scientist Donald A. Norman in an article published in the January 2004 *Scientific American* (p. 37A). "Emotion was traditionally ignored as some leftover from our animal heritage. It turns out that's not true." He goes on to cite studies in which people have suffered damage to the prefrontal lobes—the part of the brain responsible for our emotions—noting that although they remain intelligent and sensible, they no longer show emotions and cannot make decisions. "The role of emotions is to make judgments—this is good, that is bad, this is safe." He further contends that the two systems, emotions and cognition, are intertwined at a biological level, that people have emotions "to keep them safe, make them curious, and help them to learn."

Help us learn. Hot dog. Now there's a bottom-line reason to access our inner poet in science class—emotions help us learn.

Beyond that, the language of poetry helps us communicate in a complex arena of separate and not always equal specialties.

The Questioning Poem

I tell kids that mostly I write about two things— what I know and what I wonder about. That wondering is not only the first step in what we have come to call the writing process but also the first step in the scientific process.

Poets and scientists ask questions. *How could this be? Why does that happen? What follows next? How do we use our knowledge so that we can learn to predict? What is our conclusion?* Lots of questions. Also, both must have a keen eye for observation, for data collection, and for comparisons. Both must be very careful about definitive language.

What's that about? is a great source of motivation to poets, scientists, pencil tappers, and gum poppers. Kids are more inclined to find and remember the answers to what they want to know as opposed to simply what their teachers want them to know, which is why many teachers begin units with a series of questions. Casting questions in the form of a poem for classroom sharing gives a surprising kick to a reliable jump-start.

Writing a questioning poem involves four simple steps: initial inquiry, collection and cataloging of data, collaborative writing, and presentation.

◆ Share my questioning poem (or another example) on an overhead and discuss.

◆ Divide your class into groups of four to eight students.

◆ Give each group a stack of index cards and ask them to write down questions about a unit of study. (Katie's students were about to start a unit on alcohol, tobacco, and drugs.) Encourage the students to write as many questions as they can, without attribution—one question to a card. Pile the cards in the center of each group's table.

◆ Give each group a sheet of paper and ask one student to assume the role of scribe.

◆ Have the groups compile a poem using the questions written on the index cards. To do so, they will need to collect and prioritize their data and write collaboratively. Remind the writers that most scientific papers, like a lot of other writing from television sit-coms to annual reports, are collaborative efforts. People have to work together to hash things out.

◆ Ask the writers to come up with a way, as a group, to present their poem to the rest of the class. Ideas include turning it into a skit, adding rhythm, creating a song, taking turns reading various lines.

◆ Have students present their poems to the class. Two rules: 1. Everyone must participate. 2. Obey school rules. (No setting the room on fire or insulting fellow students.)

◆ Assess students' ability to collaborate and participate and their ability to formulate relevant questions based on prior (even if inaccurate) knowledge.

Katie's classroom was divided into three working groups who dubbed themselves the No Names, the Don't Knows, and the Wigglies. Naming the groups gave each an instant sense of community identity, reinforcing one of the unifying concepts of the standards—students should work more in groups (and less as individuals) to analyze and synthesize data.

Standards
Unifying concepts and processes. Combines *scientific inquiry with writing* and provides students with a *big picture* of why a given topic is important.
A. Science as inquiry. Engages students in *identifying questions that can be answered through scientific investigations*, helps students *formulate questions that are relevant and meaningful*, begins to build a *community of learners* as students collaborate, engages students in *questioning and querying other students*, and raises awareness that *ideas are to be presented in oral and/or written reports*.
F. Science in personal and social perspectives. Provides a foundation for students' *appreciation of the importance of personal health*, here as applied to the *hazards of alcohol, tobacco, and drugs*. (This can be expanded to include other standards when the exercise is used with other topics.)

Why are cigarettes so addicting?
What's in them that makes you can't stop?
Are illegal drugs sold in the store
just like pop?
Can you tell people to stop their drugs
even if they're your friends?
Is it dangerous, is it safe,
what if the friendship ends?
Are there a lot of bad drugs in this world?
If so, what for?
And here's another question we have,
how come people want more?
Do drugs affect the way you talk,
eat, sleep, and think?
Can you turn different colors with drugs—
blue, orange, or even pink?
Questions, questions are what we have,
and they never seem to stop.
Hopefully we can get some answers,
from a parent, teacher, or a cop.
                              —The No Names

Four No Names took turns reading the poem while the remaining three acted it out; the performance culminated in a dramatic conclusion in which they all ran offstage screaming like sirens.

Drugs, Alcohol, Tobacco
Why are these so bad?
Why were they invented?
To start this filthy fad?
Why do people take them
Even though it kills?
Why so many ways?
Injections, tablets, pills
Selling, buying, taking
Makes me have a rude awakening.
Why is this happening?
What should I do?
                              —The Don't Knows

The Don't Knows had a two-student rhythm section, a single reader, and three students acting out the poem.

> Who makes drugs?
> When were they cool?
> How do they kill you?
> I wish not smoking was a rule.
> What is in alcohol that makes you go nuts
> And makes you want to throw up your guts?
> When did they find out drugs are bad?
> Now I guess there [sic] not a fad.
> What's the difference between drugs and tobacco?
> I don't know, but they both make you wacko.
> So answer me this . . .
> Who makes drugs?
>
> —The Wigglies

The Wigglies had a one-student rhythm section (he beat a ruler on a book) backing up a single reader. The rest of the group, snapping their fingers, acted out certain passages. For a finale, they all held up their palms on which they had written antidrug messages.

Following the presentations (and torrents of applause) we talked a little about what poets and scientists might have in common. Some of the student responses were:

When you write, you think of different questions.

Poetry helps people find new ideas.

Poetry in science means that learning can be fun.

We get to work together in both.

One student summed up the discussion by remarking that writing a poem in science is "not just looking at the overhead and taking notes," adding, "It's better to do it than to read it in a book." The class response was immediate and unanimous— everyone agreed.

Pleased with the results of the exercise, Katie made sure to provide scientific answers in subsequent lessons to questions such as "What is it about alcohol that makes you sick?" and "How do drugs kill you?" Not only did these poems help assess students' prior knowledge, but they also put a little oil on the wheel of their curiosity.

Dreaming Up More Questions

"Stuck Here" is another model of a questioning poem (see page 99). It is a little about gravity and a lot about daydreaming. I may be going out on a limb here, but I'd venture that many students are more familiar with daydreaming than they are with gravity. But we can't cross off daydreams as useless. Any scientist or artist will tell you that daydreams about what is and what is not possible are the impetus of creative exploration.

In this exercise you can combine standards A and B with a lesson on physical, life, earth, or space science, or on the history of science, depending on your unit of study. Say today's lesson is *not* on gravity, as it is in "Stuck Here." Let's say it's on photosynthesis. Or oceans. Or microscopes. Or forest fires. Anything the kids can imagine being with or without and predict what the outcome would be. The object is to rewrite the poem, completing it with questions about the unit.

- Share the poem "Stuck Here" with students and discuss the pattern of the poem.

- Have students break into small groups and formulate questions that relate to your current unit of study. Tell them to let their imaginations run wild. What would life be like if there weren't such a thing as a skeletal system? Electricity?

- Ask them to arrange these questions using "Stuck Here" as a model, rewriting the poem complete with their personal (often misguided and fictional) questioning daydreams.

- ◆ Be sure to provide time to share the poems.

- ◆ Assess students' appreciation of the benefits of their topic and their logic in inferring what life would be like with and without it.

As I Was Saying, Precisely!

The experiment took too long. / The experiment took two hours and forty-five minutes longer than the last time.

The snowfall last night was delightful. / Four inches of snow fell last night and blanketed the bushes and trees.

Nothing wrong with a good opinion. I have plenty of them. (Don't get me started.) But if we want to use opinion words (subjective terms) in our science writing or in our poetry, we'd better be prepared to back them up with explanations. We commonly think of scientific writing as precise, given to mathematical equations and detailed descriptions and explanations. Poetry is just as demanding, challenging the poet to define subjective observations with images and comparisons.

Any time an opinion is stated in a poem, we have to define it. It is not good enough to write, "My brother is weird." Like Ed McMahon, we have to ask, "How weird is he?" Does he have a wart on his nose? The skin of a reptile? The poem "Hopeless" (see page 101) illustrates this point; it puts forward an opinion— "My dad is so stupid"—and then goes on to provide details.

Stuck Here

Today's lesson is on gravity.
If there weren't such a thing as gravity,
my feet wouldn't stick to the floor.
Instead I would rise like a stone
and fly like a pig through the door.

Open your books to page 138.
I could hit baseballs out of the park,
but I couldn't play soccer or bowl.
I guess I could maybe still rock,
but for sure I could not simply roll.

John, will you begin reading for us?
I could up-and-over-slam-dunk a house.
I could vault without a pole.
I could plow through clouds in the sky,
or I could fall up a hole.
I'd just need cruise control.

John?
"This is flying *Titanic* to ground control."
Accelerating—picking up speed . . .
destination, the South Pole.
"You're fading on me. Do you read?"

Mr. Beasley. Is your mind on gravity?
Let's just stick to the book, Mr. Beasley.
Gravity is heavy,
and you can bet that it's for real.
Look how I'm stuck to this book.
Gravity.
Bum deal.

—SARA HOLBROOK,
The Dog Ate My Homework

Standards

A. Science as inquiry. Develops students' abilities to *design and conduct a scientific investigation*, calls on students' abilities to *gather and organize data* and reach conclusions based on evidence, and helps them *recognize the relationship between explanation and evidence* as they *challenge current beliefs and concepts and provide scientific explanations as alternatives.*

B. Physical science. Provides an opportunity to *learn to examine the characteristic properties of a substance* (food).

F. Science in personal and social perspectives. Examines the *nutrients and characteristics of foods,* introduces a *systematic approach to thinking critically.*

Most opinions are a matter of perspective. Whether liver tastes bad or good is a matter for one's palate. Whether something is small or large depends on where one stands in the universe:

> Large tree.
> Small me.

> Large me.
> Small flea.

Kids tend to use broad terms for descriptions. Words like *large* and *small* or *short* or *easy* or *hard* have little or no meaning in a scientific or poetic context (hard like algebra or hard like this tabletop?).

> Huge tree.
> Puny me.

When I ask kids to rewrite a poem like this, they first believe they are being more precise by saying something like:

> Tall me.
> Minuscule flea.

Maybe the student is proud because she used a thesaurus to come up with the word *minuscule*. Unfortunately, that word tells the reader very little. Both the poet and the scientist would be looking for something more precise, more visual:

> 50-foot tree.
> 5-foot me.

> 5-foot me.
> .05-millimeter flea.

To improve scientific writing, we have to define our opinions with facts, but before we can do that, we have to be able to recognize subjective terms when we drop them in our writing. According to the science standards, "students often have the vocabulary for many aspects of health, but they often do not understand the science related to the terminology." Kids are readily able to tell us that physical exercise is good and being a couch potato is bad, but they often need some nudging to take their writing to the next level—to clarify *why* this is so.

◆ Make a spreadsheet naming a "good" food. Have students turn their papers sideways and divide them into six columns. At the top of five of the columns have them name a description or characteristic for the "good" food. (Don't define "good" as healthy or unhealthy, yummy or nasty—you're trying to teach a *good* point here.) (See Figure 4–1, where Frankie describes his good food—pie.)

◆ Share the poem "Hopeless" with students. Identify the opinion words used to describe the dad in the poem: *stupid, dumb,* and *hopeless* (sorry, Dad). Discuss how the poem defines the opinion words so that they have meaning. Practice your best imitation of Ed McMahon and ask after the each of the first two lines, *How stupid is he? How dumb is he?* This helps underscore how the poem answers these questions.

Hopeless

My dad is so stupid.
My dad is so dumb.
He calls the wrong name
when he wants me to
    come.

He calls me
Barbara–Bob–Stacey,
and I answer,
"Who?"
Then he slaps at his
    forehead
and yells,
"Number 2!"

"You're hopeless,"
I tell him,
and then he gets riled.
But what gives
when a man
does not know
his own child?

—SARA HOLBROOK,
Nothing's the End of the World

Pie	crusty	tasty	sweet	filled with tasty fruits	fattening	health benefits?
Shortening baked 450° flour butter pinch of love	sugar salt	sugar fruits gel syrup juice		Apples Pears Peach Cherry strawberry blueberry rasberry Pecan Cream	sugar calories carbs butter shortening oil milk	Quick energy high carb vitamins from fruit minerals Protein

FIG. 4–1 *Frankie's Spreadsheet*

- Have students turn to their "good food" spreadsheet and ask them to cover the name of their "good" food. Are they able to guess the food by just looking at the descriptors? Have they been specific enough or have they just listed opinions? Probably the latter. Most examples will be broadly stated and full of opinions needing definition. Such descriptors lack the "rich explanatory power" recommended for scientific writing, but they can lead the way to a meaningful learning experience—a (pardon me) "fruitful investigation" and a descriptive poem.

- Ask students to choose one of their "good foods" and list more precise descriptors. Have them title the sixth column "possible health benefits." This is where they'll need to do some research to determine what it is that makes pie (or whatever) tasty, sweet, and (sigh) fattening. *How sweet is it? What makes it sweet? What are the ingredients? How does pie get crusty? Does pie have any health benefits?*

- When students have completed the new charts, have them check to make sure they have not substituted one opinion word for another—for example, *tasty* for *delicious*. The characteristics should now explain the opinions expressed in the first spreadsheet.

- Have students use the second chart to compose a riddle poem about their chosen food. These poems should be mouthwatering. Here is sixth-grader Frankie's finished poem: The pie is no longer just "tasty," he has provided an explanation. As you read it, can you guess it is about a pie?

Baked at 450, apples and cream,
raspberry syrup, oh what a dream.
Crusty and sweet from shortening and sugar. It's a good pastry
I eat with ice cream, oh so tasty.
The only downside to this treat is all the fat,
who cares. Let's eat.

- After students have written and polished their poems, ask them to share them as a class or in small groups. Tell them to save the title for last: Can the class guess what food the poem is about before the author reveals the title?

◆ Assess the students' ability to distinguish between fact and opinion in describing the characteristics of a food, research and organize their data in a spreadsheet, and incorporate those details into a piece of creative writing, justifying their opinions with specific explanations.

Pass the Movement: Putting Motion into Words

Outside the bay window in my office, leaves mambo, geese glide high overhead, and bushes shimmy in the wind. Two cardinals are balancing themselves on the phone line with their tails, and snow is floating around absentmindedly. The world is constantly dancing.

The physical science standards state that students must not only be able to describe the characteristic properties of an object or matter but also be able to trace its movement. Putting motion into words is another challenge shared by poets and scientists. To get started, we actually need to move. (Don't worry, the initial groans will be followed by smiles and giggles.)

◆ Have the class form a big circle. Start by touching your knees with both hands, tapping your shoulders, or performing some other simple action. Have all the kids imitate your movement. Next, say "Pass"; the person to your right then changes the movement, maybe clapping his hands. Everyone mimics that movement and so on all around the circle.

◆ Have everyone return to his seat and then select three or four students to come to the front of the class.

◆ One at a time, have these students recreate their movements and have the class put the movements into words. No fair saying, "Ryan is acting crazy." The class has to describe *exactly* what Ryan is doing: "Ryan crossed his eyes and made circles

"Suit the action to the word, the word to the action...."

—WILLIAM SHAKESPEARE, *Hamlet* (1601)

Standards

A. Science as inquiry. Develops students' abilities to center on evidence rather than personal explanations, to differentiate explanation from description.

B. Physical science. Provides an opportunity for students to learn how the motions of an object can be described by its position, direction of motion, and speed.

at his temples with one finger from each hand." Not "LaTesha is acting like she is all that," but "LaTesha stood with her arms folded looking down her nose with skinny eyes."

◆ Write these observations on the board.

◆ Have each student select one of the movement descriptions and work it into a four- or five-sentence story—that is, develop a hypothesis to explain it. What could be happening to cause Ryan to do the circle thing with his fingers at his temples? What's going on that LaTesha has this attitude? Allow no more than six or seven minutes.

◆ Have students share their stories in pairs and then with the class. After the class listens to two or more stories on a motion, ask, *Which hypothesis is right?* Do the same thing with the other motions. Listen to at least two stories for each motion. Discuss the difference between evidence and interpretation.

◆ Assess students' ability to describe the motion of an object in exact detail based on evidence, not interpretation.

Katie's sixth-grade science class described three motions:

1. He shrugged his shoulders and turned palms up with bugged eyes.

2. He scratched his shoulders and his armpit.

3. She moved her hands out smoothly like she was swimming through the air.

Each of Katie's students made up a story to explain one of the motions, which were simple and yet visual enough to spark an idea. Here are a few examples:

> When John walked in from school his mom asked, "What did you do at school today." He shrugged his shoulders and turned his hands palms up with bugged eyes. His mom said, "Why do you always do this?" He did the same thing. John liked to be by himself and that is why he always shrugged his shoulders. He was very intelligent, he just didn't like school. That is the story of John.
>
> —*Kevin, Grade 6*

He shrugged his shoulders and turned palms up with bugged eyes. His mom said, who made this mess? He said, I don't know. Come on, you know what you did. No I don't. Yes you do. No I don't.

—*Nick, Grade 6*

In a straight line, she moved her hands out smoothly like she was swimming through the air. Trying to get through without a care. She was moving her hands, smoothly, like silk. She was flying, she was swimming, and then she woke up.

—*Lesley, Grade 6*

I discourage kids who want to interpret the movements—*actor 1 was giving his mom some attitude, actor 2 was acting like Monkey Boy, or actor 3 was doing a silly dance.* These types of descriptors are what we try to avoid in scientific and poetic observations because they draw conclusions that we can't know just by looking. Better to stick to the facts, describe the motion without the emotion.

Students took turns reading their stories aloud. We compared them, and I asked which was true. Was Kevin's or Nick's story true? Was Lesley's? We agreed that none of them were true and none were false, they were just speculations, interpretations of the movements that went beyond describing the evidence.

We then discussed why it is important for scientists not just to make up stories about why something is happening. It was an intense discussion about the importance of basing our observations strictly on what we see, not what we think we see.

There's a Poem in There Somewhere

Another one of our challenges as writers and scientists is sifting through tons of sand to find a few specs of gold. Mining data and honing it down to the most essential parts are skills we can practice by condensing our stories into poems.

> **Standards**
>
> A. Science as inquiry. Helps students to *think critically and logically to make the relationship between evidence and explanations* while encouraging them to *develop the ability to listen to and respect the explanations proposed by other students;* and affords them the opportunity to *describe observations, summarize, and tell other students about investigations and explanations.*

◆ Ask students to look at their stories and underline the most important words. Which words would they absolutely have to retain to describe the image (the motion) and tell the story? Have them underline the key words. The goal is to create a poem from the story that uses fewer words but maintains the movement thereby capturing an image in words.

◆ Have students copy the words over in shortened lines. Voila. A poem begins to emerge. Students can then share the before and after versions of the story/poem and begin to recognize the importance of culling their observations down to the key points.

◆ Assess students' ability to distinguish between evidence and explanation, describe movement in a visual way, and condense their writing to the most important points.

Here are the poem versions of the preceding stories.

school	shrugged	smoothly
shrugged	bugged eyes	swimming
shoulders	turned palms up	swimming
hands palms up	his mom	clouds
bugged eyes	what did you	smoothly
John	don't	silk
by himself	did	flying
intelligent	don't	swimming
didn't like school	do	woke up
—Kevin, Grade 6	don't	—Lesley,
	—Nick, Grade 6	Grade 6

The students were amazed at the poems they created out of their little made-up stories. The process of going from a factual observation to an explanation (in this case pure fiction) and then prioritizing their data to find the most important points is one that will help them in all their writing, particularly scientific writing, in which they will be asked to handle more complex issues and compounding data.

Do-It-Yourself Haiku: Just the Facts, Ma'am

Only the most polished haiku poet can capture an entire scene in seventeen syllables, but even a novice (like me) can manage to capture certain descriptive facts in that context (see page 65 for more information about haiku). Cataloging data about a subject can lead to one of these little poems. And while any one of these haiku may not paint a complete picture, when put together, they should create something that reinforces content standard learning.

The important thing about writing these poems is to stick to the truth. Later, by reorganizing the lines, you may create some chuckles or glimmers of brilliance, but start with the facts.

Katie's sixth-grade science students wrote some haiku while they were in the midst of their unit on tobacco, alcohol, and drugs. Since haiku are short, they narrowed their focus to just tobacco.

◆ Take a few minutes to brainstorm words and phrases that describe the subject. Katie's class focused on the ways in which tobacco is taken into, and its effects on, the human body.

◆ Explain the rules of haiku, perhaps writing a group poem together or showing a sample. (Three lines, five syllables, seven syllables, five syllables).

◆ Ask each student to write a haiku on the subject. Sloppy copy first.

Here are some from Katie's sixth graders:

Smoking hurts your lungs
Cigarettes can make you sick
It gives you bad breath.

Don't smoke tobacco.
Smoking is the worst for you.
Smoking can kill kids.

Nicotine is bad.
Smoking turns your teeth yellow.
Second-hand smoke kills.

Tobacco smells bad
Nicotine rots your lungs.
Make effort to stop.

Standards*

A. Science as inquiry. Requires students to use *background knowledge.*

F. Science in personal and social perspectives. Expands students' *knowledge of the risks and benefits of tobacco,* reinforces the lesson that *tobacco increases the risk of illness,* and increases understanding of the *long-term detrimental effects of smoking and chewing tobacco.*

G. History and nature of science. Helps students see *the scientific enterprise as more philosophical, social, and human* and develop a better understanding of the interactions between science and society.

As applied to a unit on tobacco; exercise could also be used to support alternate content standards.

Snakes are not slimy
Snakes are cold-blooded
    with scales
Snakes can't ride a bike.

—SARA HOLBROOK

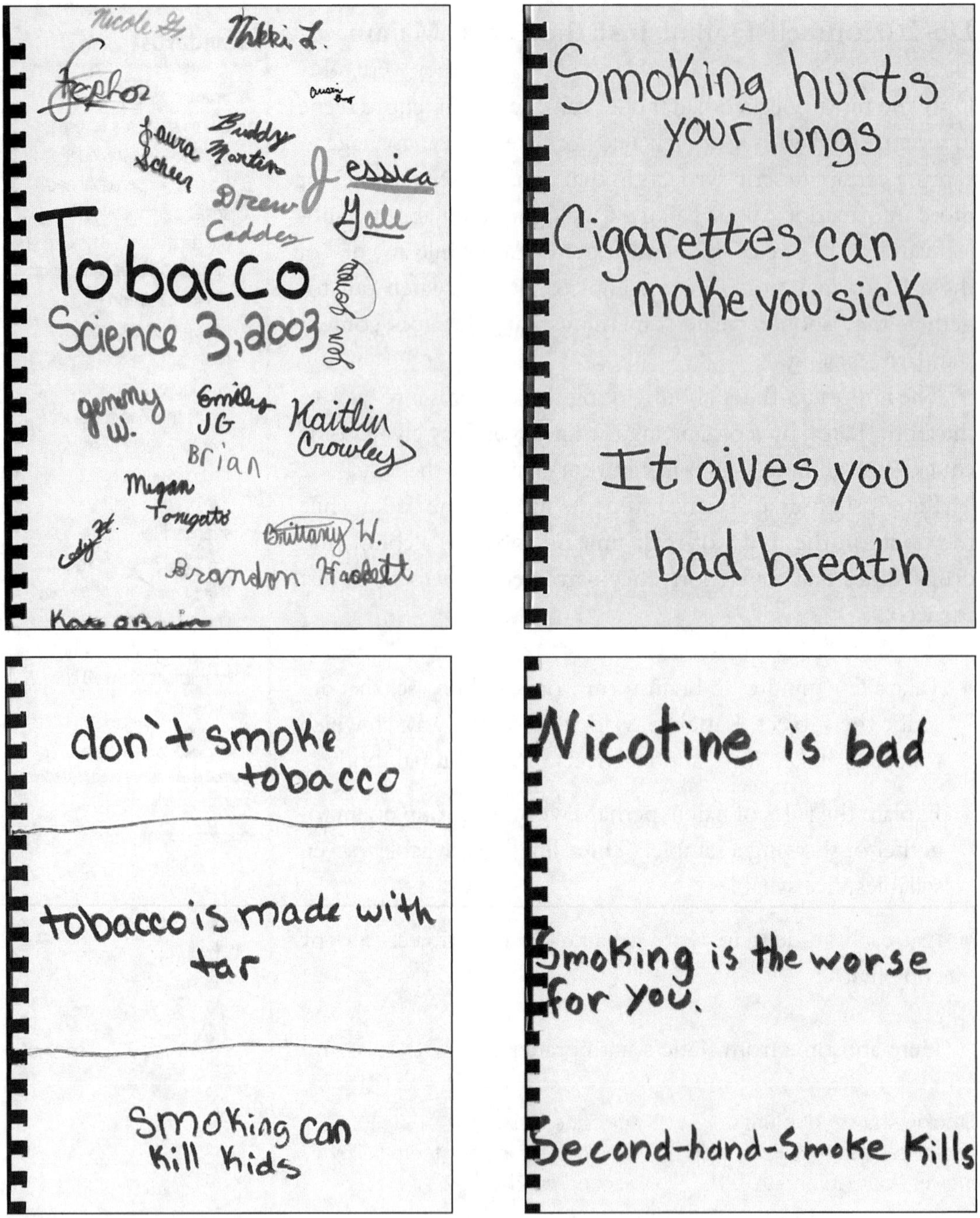

FIG. 4–2 *Tobacco Poems*

- Pass out sheets of colored construction paper and have kids fold their sheets into thirds horizontally, as if they were folding a letter to insert into an envelope.

- Have students copy one line of their poems on each third of the paper in large print using a marker or a crayon.

- Have somebody make a cover for your book of haiku. Katie's class tramped down to the library, which had a Vella binding machine. Together, they punched, assembled, and bound their class book. Then they cut the pages along the fold lines so that they were able to flip through and recombine lines into new haiku. Start to finished book product, forty minutes. Afterward, the writers each autographed the cover—because that's what authors do.

- Assess students' content knowledge as reflected in their haiku and their ability to recognize and follow a pattern.

We Are One: Becoming a "Pal of the World"

Ever crawl out of bed scratching, stiff as a bear after a four-month nap? Screech like a crow or (groan) laugh like a hyena? Nature is so much more than what's out there; it's also what's inside us. In his prose poem "Wilderness," Carl Sandburg recognizes that he has a zoo in him, that part of who he is is what he comes from. Building connections between ourselves, our fellow citizens of the natural world, and our shared history and environment is away to find our place in the world. Using Sandburg's poem as a model, kids can explore their evolution by calling on their inner animal (*grrrrrr*) and finding out they are "pals of the world."

- Share Sandburg's prose poem "Wilderness" with the class. (Rather than just reading it to them, you might have individual students each read a part.)

Standards

A. Science as inquiry. Requires students to *integrate research into creative writing* and *present evidence to support an argument.*

C. Life science. Requires students to *provide evidence of how a species moves, obtains food, reproduces, and responds to danger* based on the species' evolutionary history; although different species might look dissimilar, *the unity among organisms becomes apparent from common internal structures, similarity of their chemical processes, and evidence of common ancestry.*

Wilderness

There is a fox in me . . . a silver-gray fox . . . I sniff and guess . . . I pick things out of the wind and air . . . I nose in the dark night and take sleepers and eat them and hide the feathers . . . I circle and loop and double-cross.

There is a hog in me . . . a snout and a belly . . . a machinery for eating and grunting . . . a machinery for sleeping satisfied in the sun—I got this too from the wilderness and the wilderness will not let it go.

There is a fish in me . . . I know I came from saltblue water-gates . . . I scurried with shoals of herring . . . I blew waterspouts with porpoises . . . before land was . . . before the water went down . . . before Noah . . . before the first chapter of Genesis.

There is a baboon in me . . . clambering-clawed . . . dog-faced . . . yawping a galoot's hunger . . . hairy under the armpits . . . here are the hawk-eyed hankering men . . . here are the blond and blue-eyed women . . . here they hide curled asleep waiting . . . ready to snarl and kill . . . ready to sing and give milk . . . waiting—I keep the baboon because the wilderness says so.

There is an eagle in me and a mockingbird . . . and the eagle flies among the Rocky Mountains of my dreams and fights among the Sierra crags of what I want . . . and the mockingbird warbles in the early forenoon before the dew is gone, warbles in the underbrush of my Chattanoogas of hope, gushes over the blue Ozark foothills of my wishes—and I got the eagle and the mockingbird from the wilderness.

O, I got a zoo, I got a menagerie, inside my ribs, under my bony head, under my red-valve heart—and I got something else: it is a man-child heart, a woman-child heart: it is a father and mother and lover: it came from God-Knows-Where: it is going to God-Knows-Where—for I am the keeper of the zoo: I say yes and no: I sing and kill and work: I am a pal of the world: I came from the wilderness.

—CARL SANDBURG,
Cornhuskers (1918)

◆ Let students discuss why Sandburg chose the animals he did in this poem.

◆ Brainstorm some other animals that might be part of the zoo inside all of us.

◆ Have the students write a verse, copying Sandburg's style, describing an animal inside them.

◆ Ask students to share their poems aloud with the class or in small groups of four or five. (You might have student groups put their verses together into a collaborative poem and present them to the class.)

◆ Assess students' grasp of the notion of the interconnectedness of the world and their ability to verbalize it by relating how they identify with a certain animal.

That Was Then, This Is Now: Charting Our Growth

Sometimes I make small talk with the small-fry in the front rows before assemblies. Remember those assemblies? Ankle biters up front, pretzel legs, hands folded neatly (at least to start). I ask, "So is this the fifth grade?" They laugh and laugh. Silly poet.

Then I ask, "Would you like to be in fifth grade? For a day anyway?" Almost everyone thinks this is a great idea. Big for a day. Cool beans. But one skeptic usually shakes his head.

"Why not?"

"Fifth graders have too much homework." Or "Fifth graders have too many jobs."

While it may seem as if kids are pedal-to-the-metal toward adulthood, part of them knows (or at least suspects) that grown-up may not be as fun and free as it looks. Part of guiding kids through the dark and volatile forest of adolescence is helping them appreciate the changes in their bodies and the responsibilities that go with maturity. Behavioral choices about nutrition, drugs, exercise, sex are all part of science class because they are part of becoming adults, which, if you've watched MTV lately, appears to happen at age twelve.

Seriously, kids are faced with behavioral choices that weren't even on the map when their teachers were kids. As the standards remind us, "Middle-school students are aware of science-technology-society issues from the media, but their awareness is fraught with misunderstandings." (No kidding. Have you seen those "spring break" programs? Holy breasts and beer cans.) Naturally, we don't want kids to think adulthood is all a big party. However, the standards go on to state, "Teachers should begin developing students' understanding with concrete and personal examples that avoid an exclusive focus on problems." In other words, changes in the human body and behaviors associated with adolescence are a natural process of personal growth.

To better appreciate where we are going, it helps to chart how far we've come. Using an exercise by respected poet/educator Kenneth Koch, in *Wishes, Lies, and Dreams,* students examine changes in themselves as they cross over from childhood to adolescence and adulthood. (This exercise might serve as a good introduction to a unit on health and the body.)

◆ Have students, on their own or as a collaborative writing process, complete the following writing prompt and turn it into a poem:

> I used to be _____
> Now I am _____

I used to be short, now I am tall. I used to eat strained pears, now I eat pizza. The possibilities are personal.

Standards

C. Life science. Causes kids to examine how they *interact with one another and with their environment,* highlights the *period of development in youth [that] lends itself to human biology,* helps kids understand *the complementary nature of structure and function,* and leads to an understanding that *behavioral response is a set of actions determined in part by heredity and in part from experience.*

F. Science in personal and social perspectives. Helps *expand students' study of health* as they begin to *learn about risks and personal decisions* and helps overcome students' perception that *most factors related to health are beyond their control.*

Old Pictures

See that hole in my smile
and the pat on my head?
I was so old
I could make my own bed.

I could pull on my boots,
zipper my coat,
pick up my toys
and tie my own bows.

I am much older
since I lost that tooth,
but you want to know
the honest-to-truth?

Grown-up gets scary,
and that is a fact.
If I'd had a half-a-brain,
I'd have
put that tooth back.

—SARA HOLBROOK,
Am I Naturally This Crazy?

◆ If you make this a collaborative exercise, kids see themselves and the changes they are experiencing as typical rather than pathological, which of course is what many fear. Have kids use index cards, as many as they like, to record their *used to be/now I am* observations, and then assemble them into a group poem.

◆ Whether working independently or in small groups, it is fun to illustrate these poems with drawings or old snapshots.

◆ These poems beg for oral presentation. This develops presentation skills, builds community in the classroom, and gives you insight into students' perceptions. (You may wish to copy the poems onto transparencies and project them for performance.)

◆ Assess students' ability to acknowledge and document personal changes in themselves as they are beginning to mature.

Here is a group poem written by retained seventh graders at Gompers Secondary School in San Diego:

I used to like toys,
Now I like music.
I used to be simple,
Now I am confusing.
I used to like Barbies
Now I like make-up.
I used to look at pictures,
Now I can read.
I used to follow,
Now I can lead.
I used to be happy
Now I am sad.
I used to be good
Now I am bad.
I used to like turkey
Now I like ham.
Mama used to hold me
Now I hold my own hand.
I used to be scared

But now I am brave.
I used to be scared
But now I am brave.

Since most of these students were native Spanish speakers, we also wrote a version of this poem in Spanish for an assembly performance before the rest of the school. The kids performed it to a we-will-we-will-rock-you rhythm, accompanied by a *stomp, stomp, clap* beat. The translation stimulated a lot of talk about how exact translations often don't create the right rhythms, a lesson translators have been struggling with since the days of cave drawings. These kids were not accustomed to receiving a lot of positive attention in school, but when they busted loose with this poem in Spanish, it brought the house down. Even the toughest of the tough kids in the audience was stomping in enthusiastic support.

Katie's sixth graders at Bay Middle School were beginning their unit on the human body when they did this exercise. We talked about the changes they were experiencing as they entered adolescence. To widen their perspective, I noted on the board some alternatives to the verb *to be: to like, to watch, to hate, to play, to wear.* One of the poems they created and performed (with rhythm, raucous applause, and hilarity) follows:

I used to lock people in the playhouse and leave them,
Now I play with them.

I used to have nap time,
Now I have band.

I used to swim in the baby pool,
Now I swim in the big pool.

I used to have few friends,
Now I have new friends.

I used to go everywhere with my mom,
Now I don't.

I used to go to the store,
Now I stay at home.

I used to watch *Sesame Street*,
Now I watch *Sports Center*.
—Austin, Grade 6

Feelings Make Me Real: Getting to the Nitty-Gritty in Drug Units

People use alcohol and drugs to change the way they feel. Ca-sual users try drugs to feel different, addicts need them to feel normal. Science teachers educate kids about the hazards of al-cohol and drugs, working head to head against deep-pocketed corporations spending big bucks to urge the public to "take this, you'll feel better." We are bombarded by media assaults designed to make us believe we are not in control of our own emotions, that we can feel good all the time if we take this pur-ple, green, or blue pill. Of course no one feels good all the time, and part of any drug education unit is helping kids understand that we need to accept our feelings, even the negative ones, as part of the natural flow.

I worked as a community education coordinator for the Cleveland branch of the National Council on Alcohol and Drug Dependence during the 1980s. We were designing drug edu-cation units for middle schools and fighting to get drug educa-tion into elementary schools. The units were bite-size and very rudimentary: a little pretest, a little education, a posttest to mea-sure the learning. We designed the test to be open-ended, just simple fill-in-the-blanks:

◆ What I know about alcohol is _____.

◆ What I know about drugs is _____.

The pretest answers showed an incredible media influence: *What I know about alcohol is it's like a party, it makes you happy, it comes in brown bottles.* Then every once in a while would come a response like this: *What I know about alcohol is that when my brother drinks it makes my mom cry.*

Students come to school with remarkable differences in their perceptions of drugs and alcohol, which is no news to a science teacher, I realize. Poetry is the language of feeling. Love, hate, remorse, joy, anxiety, stress, hopelessness, and just plain boredom are all reasons to write poetry—or to take drugs. Based on personal experience, I recommend poetry as an antidrug, an alternative way of dealing with feelings rather than trying to mask or medicate them.

In a poem written over a century ago (see sidebar), Dunbar talks about masking who he really is, wearing a smile to cover a torn and bleeding heart. A word about the poet. His father was an escaped slave and Civil War veteran. He grew up in Dayton, Ohio, where his mother was the laundry woman for none other than the family of Orville and Wilbur Wright, who were his lifelong friends and supporters. The only African American in his high school, he was by all accounts a brilliant student, but the best job he could find after graduation was as an elevator operator. (I have always admired this poem and was familiar with the poet, but it was not until I reviewed his biography for this book that I discovered he died at thirty-three from complications from alcoholism.)

> **We Wear the Mask**
>
> We wear the mask that grins and lies,
> It hides our cheeks and shades our eyes—
> This debt we pay to human guile;
> With torn and bleeding hearts we smile,
> And mouth with myriad subtleties.
>
> Why should the world be overwise,
> In counting all our tears and sighs?
> Nay, let them only see us, while
> We wear the mask.
>
> We smile, but, O great Christ, our cries
> To thee from tortured souls arise.
> We sing, but oh the clay is vile
> Beneath our feet, and long the mile;
> But let the world dream otherwise,
> We wear the mask!
>
> —PAUL LAURENCE DUNBAR (1895)

◆ Introduce this poem along with a little history about the poet. Can students imagine why Dunbar masked his feelings? Can they see that this is a universal instinct going back generations and not just something invented by generation X, Y, or Z? How does this relate to the expression "putting on your game face"? (If you think this poem is too complex for your students, use "Popular" as a model.)

◆ Ask students to think of a time when they masked their feelings, showing an outside that did not match the inside, and to use that experience to write a poem.

◆ Have students share their poems aloud with a partner. You may ask for volunteers to share poems aloud, but don't force anyone. Kids should feel free to write about personal feelings without fear of being exposed.

◆ Assess students' ability to acknowledge and label their feelings and to identify a time when their inside did not match their outside.

◆ Ask students whether they ever hide behind a smile in order to be more likeable. Can students identify with this kind of people pleasing? Have them think of a time when they couldn't or wouldn't use their voice because they were trying to be popular and turn that into a poem.

◆ Revealing poems like this are meant to be shared, but in a gentle way. Have students first share their poems with partners and then ask for volunteers. Or pass around a sign-up sheet. Once the ball gets rolling, more and more students will join in, but sharing shouldn't be a kick-in-the-pants venture.

◆ Assess students' appreciation for the range of human emotion and feeling and their ability to portray those feelings using descriptive, visual language.

Am I Naturally This Crazy?

Nature or nurture, we all are unique. Some links to ancestry are in our DNA, others we inherit the hard way—by listening, copying, learning from the people around us. Some of those people are blood relatives, others may include the guy next door who taught you how to throw a football. Whatever the reason, and whatever the result, each of us is mixed from a unique recipe.

Writing a poem about inherited characteristics can lead to a discussion of nature versus nurture as kids begin to study reproduction and heredity. Kids are prone to looking in the mirror and asking themselves: Is this normal? Am I an aberration of the species? Am I naturally this crazy, *is it something in my genes?*

According to the science standards: "Concerning heredity, younger middle-school students tend to focus on observable traits, and older students have some understanding that genetic material carries information." The sixth graders in Katie's class seemed to be aware of both heredity and behavior, judging by their poems. They took to this assignment like free candy, all intent on composing poems that testified to their uniqueness.

◆ Share "Blueprints?" with students. You may want to also share the poem "Labels" (see Chapter 5, page 148). Discuss how we all have a unique recipe inside.

◆ Ask students to make two columns on a piece of paper. In the first column have them list family members or significant people in their lives (like that neighbor with the football) who have made a contribution to who they are. In the second column, have them list what those people gave them.

◆ Ask them to use the lists of data to compose a poem that reveals their unique recipe.

Blueprints?

Will my ears grow long as Grandpa's?
What makes us look like kin?
Tell me where'd I get long eyelashes
and where'd I get my chin?

Where'd I get my ice cream sweet tooth
and this nose that wiggles when I talk?
Where'd I get my dizzy daydreams
and my foot-rolling, side-step walk?

Did I inherit my sense of humor
and these crooked, ugly toes?
What if I balloon like Uncle Harry
and have to shave my nose?

How long after I start growing
until I start to shrink?
Am I going to lose my teeth
some day?
My hair?
My mind?
Do you think
I'll be tall or short or thin
or bursting at the seams?
Am I naturally this crazy?
Is it something in my genes?

I'm more than
who I am,
I'm also
who I'm from.
It's a scary speculation—
Who will I become?

—SARA HOLBROOK,
Am I Naturally This Crazy?

- Ask for volunteers to share their poems. (There was no doubt that the kids in Katie's class wanted to share these poems—they were jumping out of their seats to volunteer.) It might also be fun to illustrate them with family photos on posters or in PowerPoint presentations.

- Assess students' ability to recognize that they have inherited characteristics, some genetic and some behavioral.

Student Samples

Audrey's list (see Figure 4–3) of contributing people was long, evidence of an extended family with whom she is very close. Her poem is very comprehensive—she makes an effort to include everyone.

FIG. 4–3 *Audrey's List of Contributing People*

There are a lot of things
that make up the
recipe of me.
My dad's from Ireland
and my mom's from Italy.
The first word I ever said
was Grandpa Bob's first name.
He also gave me crafting skills
and then you know what came?
His brother Jack has funny ears.
My teachers taught me to fight
through my tears.
Grandpa John taught me to golf
Uncle Jay taught me to ski.
My Great Aunt gave me my name
my dog taught me responsibility.
Uncle Peter gave me computer smarts
my brother taught me theater arts.
My dad gave me a curved pinky toe
my reading skills
and the right way to go.
I have brown hair
and brown eyes
those both came from my mother's side.
My brother sent on
his growing pains.
I have nothing more
that I want to gain.
I am part of
a great family tree
made just by us
The B_____ family.

Andy told me and his table group that his eyes (which he got from his mother's side of the family) are unique, blue with orange specs:

Eyes of blue and orange
That tell me who you are
So that I can spot a Schaffer
Whether near or far. . . .

Everyone came up close to look; it was a genetically inspired teachable moment.

Peter's recipe was short and succinct, but still has teachable elements to it. What was learned? What was inherited?

My dad is comedy
My mom is looks
And my stepmom
taught me how to cook
My brother always wears a hat
So do I
How 'bout that?

Jacob took the recipe idea literally and included a "cupful of Jacob" illustration:

FIG. 4–4 *Jacob's Blueprint Poem*

As I See It: The Snapshot Poem

I don't fish. I don't bait hooks (yish). I don't cast about with anything longer than a pencil. But often, I do go fishing with my friend. He pulls out an occasional small-mouthed bass, and I pull out an occasional poem. I wrote "Channel Surfing" sitting in a canoe in Maine, observing the action in the water beside me. I didn't write about the sun reflecting on the river that day, or the grasses waving at me from the riverbed. I just focused on those water bugs and their jerky movements.

The goal of this exercise in observation is for your students to write a poem about one single, natural thing they've seen— maybe no bigger than a water bug. A poem is a snapshot, it is not a whole movie. If kids have trouble with this concept, take a few snapshots and write from those.

This exercise helps kids narrow their focus, an important element in good writing, and it also hones their observational skills as they search the environment for specific materials and properties. When they look at the world with a poet's eye, kids start to see details that they may not have noticed yet on their slide to adulthood. Scientists need to be able to describe objects in terms of their observable properties (state of matter, size, shape, color, and texture).

◆ Share "Inside Outside Inside" with students. Discuss the three different points of view and what details are evident from each.

◆ Take the class outside to find a subject on which to focus.

◆ Ask them to write down observations from three points of view.

◆ Have them turn the observations into a three-verse poem, each verse documenting one of the three points of view. Ask them to incorporate as many details as possible. Discourage the use of adjectives such as *beautiful, glorious,* or *yucky.* These

---

Channel Surfing

Water bugs
chasing their tails.
Slower than minnows,
faster than snails.
Scooping up specs
for their dinners.
Without destination,
without hesitation,
they circle around and around.
Never in depth,
just surface skimmers.

—SARA HOLBROOK

Standards*

G. History and nature of science. *Provides background for developing and understanding scientific inquiry, provides an opportunity for student scientists to formulate and test their explanations of nature using observation (for most major ideas in science, there is much experimental and observational confirmation),* demonstrates that different scientists will draw different conclusions from the same data, *and demonstrates that open communication is integral to the process of science.*

Beyond this, every science standard lists keen observational skills on the part of student scientists as a learning objective.

tell us nothing as scientists or poets. The meaning is in the details.

◆ Share these poems aloud or in writing with illustrations. Use them to demonstrate that though the entire class had the same data available (the school yard, woods, or parking lot), the student scientists made different observations. By communicating with one another, we get a more comprehensive picture of what is really out there.

◆ Assess students' ability to view a scene from three different points of view and record their observations in visual language.

Combustible Poetry

A student asked me once, "So what is it like being a poet? You walk in the woods all day and write poems about it?" I tried explaining that I also had to do the dishes and empty the cat box the same as everyone else, but I could see he wasn't buying it. And while I do spend some time outdoors collecting data, I must confess that most of my ideas come from right inside the house. There is a prevailing belief that poets are somehow "otherworldly" figures (sometimes promoted by poets themselves) who see what others cannot and then obsess about it, breaking out in poems instead of hives like the rest of the population. The fact is, we all share the same planet, have the same viruses in our water supply, and stash the same toxins under the kitchen sink. Everyone has equal access to the textures, fumes, and effervescence known as inspiration.

Poet Michael Salinger found just such an inspiration on the back of a familiar household product during the fall of 2001 when he, along with the rest of us, was struggling to understand the disasters at the New York World Trade Center, the Pentagon, and that pitted, scorched cornfield in Pennsylvania. He produced a poem by rewriting the warning label on a can of spray paint. This is a terrific exercise that teaches figurative language while providing a lesson on the risks and benefits of common chemicals.

♦ Introduce the concept of this exercise by reading Salinger's poem. Ask students if they recognize the pattern of the language in the poem, how and why it sounds familiar.

♦ Ask students to bring in some chemical warning labels from home (no hazardous materials, please, just the labels or empty containers).

♦ The next day brainstorm a list of words that might be used in rewriting the warnings. Are they combustible? What else is combustible? love? friendship? anger? Does the warning label contain acidic substances? What else burns like acid? fear? anxiety? How or why are these potentially dangerous? What are the trade-offs?

♦ Ask students to choose one of these words (or another, if a better one presents itself) and use that word to write a poem incorporating the language of the warning label, substituting the word for the name of the product. Tell them they may

Standards

E. Science and technology. Helps raise awareness that *perfectly designed solutions do not exist,* that *all technological solutions have trade-offs, such as safety;* that technological advances have restraints, such as environmental protection, human safety, and aesthetics; and that *technological solutions have intended benefits and unintended consequences.*

F. Science in personal and social perspectives. Demonstrates *that products, processes, technologies, and inventions of a society can result in pollution and environmental degradation and may involve some level of risk to human health and to the survival of other species* and helps students realize that *maintaining environmental health involves establishing or monitoring quality standards related to use of soil, water, and air.*

911

hate is extremely flammable
its vapors may cause flash fire
hate is harmful if inhaled
keep hate away from heat, sparks, and flame
do not breath the vapors of hate
wash thoroughly after using hate
if you accidentally swallow hate
get medical attention

prejudice is an eye and skin irritant
its vapors are harmful
do not get prejudice in eyes
or on clothing
prejudice is not recommended for use
by persons with heart conditions
if prejudice is swallowed, induce vomiting
if prejudice comes in contact with skin,
remove clothing and wash skin
if breathing is affected, get fresh air
    immediately

violence is harmful if absorbed through the
    skin
keep violence out of the reach of children
do not remain in enclosed areas
where violence is present
remove pets and birds from the vicinity of
    violence
cover aquariums to protect from violence
drift and run-off from sites of violence
may be hazardous
this product is highly toxic
exposure to violence may cause
injury or death.

—MICHAEL SALINGER,
Neon

riff a little on the subject, like a jazz musician, find a theme and let it repeat itself. The warning label is a basis for poems, a starting place, not a formula designed to hold students back. They should feel free to embellish.

- Ask students to share their poems and talk about the risks and benefits of the chemicals. Have them read the labels and describe the products. Post the labels and products to foster continuing discussion.

- Assess students' ability to read and comprehend the chemical warnings on household products, recognize the risks and benefits of the chemicals, and incorporate this knowledge into a poem through the use of figurative language.

Social Studies
and Poetry

And Justice for All

The thing about poets is that what we know is mostly what we make up. The thing about social studies textbooks is that they have all the answers. Nobody's allowed to make that stuff up. Are they?

As a student in the sixties, I thought social studies was pretty clear-cut. It was my job to absorb historical facts, trace rivers, memorize countries and their capitals, and parrot the facts back on command. Overall, it was about as interesting as having the host of *Jeopardy* over for dinner and forgetting to tell him not to bring his index cards—who can warm up to a know-it-all? It wasn't until I got out of school that I realized social studies involves a great deal of controversy about what really took place. Not all historians agree with the scorekeepers. History scholars add up all kinds of disputed facts and come to different conclusions about such poster events as the launching and landing of Christopher Columbus, the first human being to reach the South Pole, and who invented the radio. (No need to get into these controversies here, but it helps to agree that there is disagreement among scholars. Okay?)

But social studies is not all about history. Turns out that while dodging media snipers and in between bus and hall duty, teachers have four sets of national standards to fold into the ten recommended thematic strands of the social studies pie—history,

Not a flagpole, pointing heavenward
with shining surety.
Not
any one set of colors
jerked cleanly up and down.
Not golden-crusted apple pie.
Not
a gray pin-striped uniform.
Not
anybody's mom.
No.
If there is a metaphor
for democracy
it is a mud-wrestling match
grit in the eyes
feet a-flying—
your ear in my teeth.
And the future?
The future belongs to the muckers
still willing to get their hands
dirty,
who roll up their sleeves
to show their colors.

—SARA HOLBROOK

economics, civics, and geography. Social studies teachers get the educational prize for multitasking. I have wrapped writing lessons around the social studies standards to help you meet your goals, but I have to say, of all the content areas, social studies were the most complicated to try to deal with. I also researched the standards in economics, history, civics, and geography in addition to related standards in several states to make sure that I understood the foundation of the more broadly stated social studies standards. Who knew that the art of studying people, places, and things could be this complex!

Okay, I admit to doodling my way through a lot of history (when was that?), geography (where was that?), civics (why was that?), and economics (what *is* that?) lessons over the years. You know students like me—I came to class with a notebook (I was always a good citizen that way), dutifully opened it up on command, doodled pictures of trees and hearts through the lecture, closed the book at the bell, and filed out of the room in an orderly fashion. I had mastered how to go with the flow. After all, what counted was that I'd memorized the boldface facts in the textbook, right? That I could choose *(a)*, *(c)*, or *all of the above* every other Tuesday. It's just possible that by devoutly following this path I may have missed a few controversies mentioned by teachers while I was busy trying to look interested. I admit that.

Oh, I remember the big controversies like the Crusades (complete with those cool heavy metal outfits) and World Wars I and II. What I don't remember is being told that there are ongoing (yes, folks, even today) arguments over our historical recordkeeping about social and political events that make fabrications by the executives of Enron look like copycat crimes. If a textbook told me that Betsy Ross made the first flag; the Moors were brutes; and the Nina, Pinta, and Santa Maria were the first crafts to cross the Atlantic east to west, I only had one question: "Is this going to be on the test on Tuesday?"

This is a dirty shame. I was duped. I was duped into thinking all this historical social and political stuff was just a collection of dead facts. Social studies is not about dead stuff at all; it is about change. And at the heart of every change are folks who want the change and folks who like things just the way they are, thank you.

Conflicts. Presented with a good catfight, students will gather to watch the fur fly. It's human nature. Unfortunately, many textbook images, the purpose of which is (I presume) to engage students' interest, are about as interesting and relevant as calendar shots of cats—sappy and boring. So how about introducing a unit with a poem? "In fourteen hundred and ninety-two, Columbus sailed the ocean blue" is much more engaging than

I was in college when students abandoned sockhops and pep rallies and took up marching against the Vietnam War. I remember arguing with my father, a purpleheart, silver-star veteran of World War II and Korea, that war was a waste of our natural resources (young men included) and (stupidly) thinking my generation was the first to take to the streets to object to armed combat. I honestly thought we'd invented it, along with rebellion against our parents. Oh, sure, there had been some sentimental moms during the Civil War who weren't all that keen on sending their boys to the front, but that seemed pretty natural. Moms are like that. But our cause seemed more noble, more informed—innovative. (Everyone deserves a little slack for the crime of thinking like a nineteen-year-old.)

And then in my twenties I sat down with a little book of poetry by Robert Service, *Rhymes of a Red Cross Man*, published in 1916. You'll remember this guy as the one who wrote those immortal (i.e., frequently anthologized) words, "A bunch of the boys were whoopin' it up at the Malamute Saloon." Like most poets, only his most politically benign poems have made it into language arts textbooks. In the middle of reading the book, I called a friend on the phone. "Did you know that there were war protesters in England before World War I?" I asked. The answer was, "There were?" It's always reassuring to know one is not alone in one's ignorance.

ol' Chris C. in a disco pose, one hand pointed skyward like some John Travolta wannabee. Or how about assessing a student's knowledge of geography terms or social injustice on the basis of a poem he or she has written on the subject?

As a former public relations executive, I can tell you with professional assurance that the best way to get the attention of folks is to present them with a controversy. Stories about a ton of new books being delivered to the library won't make the news even on a slow day. A story about one Harry Potter book being banned in Des Moines makes the cover of the *New York Times*. Controversy sells. And if the controversy is personal? If it has a "local angle"? Bull's-eye. Even the doodlers take notice.

And nothing gets a poet's pen twitching quite as quickly as a good controversy. At the heart of every change or conflict in the written history of this world has been some bothersome poet spouting off on one side or the other. Whatever the topic, some poet was scratching out a contemporaneous personal angle for posterity. The personal quality of a poem makes all those dates and events not only more interesting but more memorable. Poems are letters and snapshots from the past—"original source documents"; they're like reading someone else's mail versus reading a telephone directory. And memorable is a definite advantage when test time rolls around.

And guess what? The barn door is still open. Today's poets reserve the right to shoulder their ball-pointed weapons and fire a few words at controversies of the past—that's right, to make stuff up based on the arguable data. Kind of like that drawing of the Vikings someone painted in the nineteenth century. What are the odds that the poets will do any worse in their fabrications than what has appeared in textbooks over the years? I just learned, reading an airplane magazine last week, that some cat named Pearce in New Zealand flew an airplane about eight months before the Wright Brothers staked their claim at Kitty Hawk. Or so says his niece. Which story is true? Heck if I know.

New dinosaurs turn up all the time. Turns out that social studies is not like *Jeopardy* entirely; more like *Dragnet*. The facts and figures are definitely not all in.

Please understand I am not suggesting that we throw out textbooks in favor of waxing poetical. I'm watching my words carefully here, worried that I run the risk of being reported to the Centers for Disease Control and Prevention or some other government agency for debunking the Wright Brothers. That is *not* my intention.

I *am* suggesting that we can employ some poetic first-person accounts of historical events to create a bigger educational "bang" that students won't be as likely to buck. Poems are the voices of ordinary folks, often writing in reaction to world events, worth remembering not to the exclusion of our heroes (bicycle makers included) but in addition to them. Further, if we use content knowledge to create our own poetry, we put knowledge into action—the best route to making it part of our permanent record.

The national social studies standards call for students to identify who was involved in key events, what happened, where it happened, what events led to the developments, and what consequences followed. They are organized into ten strands and partitioned by grade level: early, middle, and high school. Language from the standards linked to the exercises within this chapter, including goals from both the early and middle grades, is set in italics.

   I. Culture: Social studies programs should include experiences that provide for the study of *culture and cultural diversity*.

 II. Time, continuity, and change: Social studies programs should include experiences that provide for the study of *the ways human beings view themselves in and over time*.

III. People, places, and environments: Social studies programs should include experiences that provide for the study of *people, places, and environments.*

IV. Individual development and identity: Social studies programs should include experiences that provide for the study of *individual development and identity.*

V. Individuals, groups, and institutions: Social studies programs should include experiences that provide for the study of *interactions among individuals, groups, and institutions.*

VI. Power, authority, and governance: Social studies programs should include experiences that provide for the study of *how people create and change structures of power, authority, and governance.*

VII. Production, distribution, and consumption: Social studies programs should include experiences that provide for the study of *how people organize for the production, distribution, and consumption of goods and services.*

VIII. Science, technology, and society: Social studies programs should include experiences that provide for the study of *relationships among science, technology, and society.*

IX. Global connections: Social studies programs should include experiences that provide for the study of *global connections and interdependence.*

X. Civic ideals and practices: Social studies programs should include experiences that provide for the study of the *ideals, principles, and practices of citizenship in a democratic republic.*

These are good goals. The goals are not the problem. The problem is the doodlers. The kids with their notebooks opened in class and their minds somewhere out in the parking lot because they are operating under the false notion that social studies is a collection of dead facts. Poetry offers the potential to engage more of these drifters.

But as a teacher you have to cover 400 years this semester. Holding up the broken leg of your desk is a thick binder of state and national standards, right? Who has time for controversies?

Well, in the words of every social studies teacher whose lesson plan ever fell victim to a student's mindless illustrations, "We've got a lot to cover. Let's move on."

Narrowing the Focus

Lots of times we tell kids to think big—the sky's the limit. In poetry we think small. Many well-meaning social studies teachers think they are doing a good thing when they ask kids to write poems about "the Civil War." This exercise has been known to produce some of *the worst* poetry ever to cross the page. And worse yet, the teacher who assigns writing the poems has to *read* them. If you want to write about the Civil War, you would be hard-pressed to get the information into a single book, let alone a poem. One could fill a library. People have.

If you were to write about one Civil War battle, you might be able to in a short story or a play. But if you write about one moment—maybe you look at a picture of the face of a dead soldier, realize that he was only seventeen years old—that's when you can write a poem. A poem turns on just a moment.

How many of us have been assigned to write an essay entitled "What I Did on My Summer Vacation"? If we were to write a poem about our summer vacation, we would narrow the topic to one moment—maybe the skin-shock of diving into the city pool on a scorching day. My favorite example of a poem of this type is by Countee Cullen, an African American poet writing around the turn of the twentieth century.

Incident

Once riding through old Baltimore
Heart filled, head filled with glee.
I saw a Baltimorian
        Was looking straight at me.

Now, I was eight and somewhat small,
But he was no whit bigger.
And so I smiled and he
Poked out his tongue
And called me nigger.

I saw the whole of Baltimore,
From May until December.
Of all the things that happened there,
That's all that I remember.

The poet spent the summer (and fall) of his eighth year in Baltimore. Writing as an adult, this is all that he is able to recall from that period of time. But this poem captures a moment not only in the poet's history but also in our nation's history. Part of what makes it so strong is what it doesn't say. It doesn't talk about the horrors of slavery or racism or how cruel children can be to one another. It doesn't try to squeeze four hundred years of injustice into twelve lines. Yet we come away with a deeper insight into all of these issues because the poet is able to capture and relate that one moment of insult.

In my travels to schools, one theme remains constant with the kids I talk to—to a person, they go out of their way to tell me they are different. "I'm not like those other kids, I'm different." And so they are. Each and every one of them. Personal identity and individual development are key components of our study of peoples and cultures of the world. If we are going to embrace the concept that different people and scholars describe time periods and events in different ways, we must first be able to identify our personal viewpoint. Poetry is good for this.

This exercise begins as a class discussion and ends with writing a poem reflecting a personal experience. It is naturally engaging for kids because it combines two of their greatest areas of interest—themselves and their friends.

◆ Ask students to think of some things they did during a specific period of time, say, last summer. Let many kids relate their memories—camp, city pool, sports, trip to grandma's, and so on.

◆ Next, ask them to recall something they did during a different time period, say, the summer before. Answers will be sketchier.

◆ Now ask them to think back three years. Do they remember anything from, say, the summer after first grade? Many will shake their heads no. One or two will have a specific memory.

◆ Focus on one student's recollection, perhaps "I went to my cousin's house for two weeks." Press the student for more details. You are looking for one memorable moment, an "incident" that is the poem within the story. The conversation might go something like this:

> "What do you remember about those two weeks?"
> "One day we went to Sea World."
> "What do you remember about that day?"
> "We had to park way far away from the entrance gate."
> "What do you remember about that?"
> "It was so hot that the parking lot burned up through my sneakers."
> "Was there one moment that sticks out in your mind?"
> "Yeah. After we walked all the way to the gate, I had to walk all over the park, and then at the end I sat down and cried because I didn't want to walk all the way back to the car."
> "Do you remember where you were, what that felt like?"
> "Yeah, I just sat down on this rock and cried. I was so tired I couldn't move."

And there it is. That moment, the moment of complete exhaustion, is the most memorable, and therein lies the poem.

Finding a poem within a story is like pouring a lot of words into a funnel; the last, most specific detail that drips out is the point of a poem.

◆ Ask the rest of the class to reiterate the details, and list the major facts on the board or an overhead.

◆ Number the facts from the broadest detail to the most specific.

◆ Copy the details in that order to create a "funnel" poem:

> In the summer after first grade I spent two weeks at my cousin's
> One day we went to Sea World
> We walked forever
> I was too tired to walk to the car
> I cried.

◆ Tell the students they are going to write their own personal history funnel poem. First get them to focus on a memory using an exercise from Natalie Goldberg's book *Writing Down the Bones*. Tell them to do a two- to three-minute freewrite beginning with the words *I remember*. The only rule is that they are to keep their pens moving, no matter what, for the designated time. If they get stuck, they are to write *I remember* again.

◆ Have them share and discuss their stories with partners.

◆ Have students, working individually, turn their stories into a numbered list of events.

◆ Have them use this list of events to create their own funnel poem. These lists won't necessarily *look* like funnels, but the lists will behave like a funnel as students direct the writers to the details that most stand out in their memories.

◆ If you wish, ask students to illustrate these poems with a family photograph or hand-drawn picture, reinforcing the point that this is a "snapshot" memory.

- As an added lesson, you may wish to narrow the time frame to the past year, the past summer holiday, or even yesterday. "Yesterday" is a day in history and, certainly, some yesterdays are more memorable than others. Comparing funnel poems will demonstrate that no matter what the event, there will be different perspectives.

- Assess students' ability to zero in on a specific moment in time by prioritizing events in a personal narrative.

From Personal Historical Narrative to Poem: Bulls Eye!

Stories have a more rambling gait than poems do. Stories meander, pause dramatically, then deadhead in distracted directions, jerked back into focus by the words *as I was saying*. Poets and historians are burdened with rendering such narratives down to a few choice words. This process is about as clean and neat as condensing four hundred years of history into four months, minus snow days and pep rallies. It ain't all that easy. Students must be able to identify and summarize key aspects of events.

This exercise is adapted from an Australian theater game I learned at a Keystone reading conference a couple of years back. The game was called "Fortunately/Unfortunately." The teacher had her students stand in a circle and take turns jumping into it while making up a new twist to the story line beginning with either *fortunately* or *unfortunately*. This is also a brilliant and dynamic way to summarize—a frequent assignment on proficiency tests.

Any historical event can be summarized by the following broad-brush formula:

Topic sentence.

Explanatory sentence.

Ten Thematic Strands in Social Studies

II. Time, continuity, and change. Helps students gain experience with sequencing to establish a sense of order and identify and use key concepts such as chronology, causality, change, conflict, and complexity to explain, analyze, and show connections among patterns of historical change and continuity.

Unfortunately, . . .

Fortunately, . . .

Finally, . . .

- ◆ Put the pattern on the board or on an overhead, then walk the students through it one sentence at a time.

- ◆ Have students put the date at the top of a piece of paper as a title to their story and then write their own historical narratives about their morning following the pattern. Narratives will include missing toothbrushes, brothers who won't get out of bed, and near misses at the bus stop. Not everyone's life will be as boring as Debbie (see next paragraph) saw hers that spring day. One student I was working with awoke to a scorpion in her shoe!

- ◆ Ask the students to underline the most important words in their summary narratives.

- ◆ Finally, have the students make a list of the underlined words. This should read like a poem version of the narrative (see Figure 5–1).

Version 1

My <u>dog</u> <u>ran</u> away This morning.
He <u>ran</u> <u>out the door</u> as I was getting in my car.
Unfortunately <u>he</u> <u>runs</u> <u>fast</u>
Fortunately I'm <u>smarter</u> than he is 35
Finally I <u>tricked him into</u> <u>the car.</u>

dog ran
out door
he runs fast
I'm smarter
Tricked him into car.

<u>13</u>

FIG. 5–1 *Historical Narrative Poem*

- Discuss the fact that while each single perspective is accurate, no single perspective can be a totally accurate depiction of that day. For an additional model, you may wish to write your own version of Debbie's poem from the teacher's perspective (grin).

- Assess students' ability to follow the pattern and their understanding of how history reconstructs multiple visions of the past to develop a historical perspective.

From Gompers Secondary School in San Diego came this inspiration:

> I got to school and when [sic] to first period.
> Then I went to second period.
> Unfortunately it was boring.
> Fortunately it's over.
> Finally lunch.
>   —Debbie, Grade 7

Without meandering by the lockers or in the parking lot, Debbie was able to summarize her morning into a little story. Next, she went from her story to a poem by underlining the most important single words or phrases in her story.

> I got to school and when [sic] to *first period*.
> Then I went to *second period*.
> Unfortunately it was *boring*.
> Fortunately it's *over*.
> Finally *lunch*.

From this, Debbie was able to make a poem about her morning:

My Poem

first period
second period
boring
over
LUNCH

Here's a story revised into a poem from Katie's sixth-grade social studies class:

When I woke up my cat's sleepy face was
right in front of me.
Then I got dressed and brushed my teeth.
Unfortunately I fell down the steps.
Fortunately I didn't get hurt.
Finally I ate breakfast and went to school.
—Julia, Grade 6

Woke up
cat's sleepy face in front of me
dressed, brushed teeth
down the steps
not hurt
ate breakfast
school.
—Julia, Grade 6

Fortunately none of us lives in a vacuum; unfortunately . . . ditto. Once we have put ourselves in the picture—the picture being the entire course of human events—we can start to appreciate the importance of perspective in the retelling of these events. The fortunately/unfortunately model can be applied to almost any event. Take Pearl Harbor:

The Japanese bombed the United States in 1941.
They bombed a place called Pearl Harbor in Hawaii.
Unfortunately, the United States was caught unaware; many died and ships were sunk.
Fortunately, not all the ships were in the harbor.
Finally, we were at war with Japan.

Of course—this is not the only perspective, right? The introduction to the standards says we must "develop the habits of mind that historians and scholars in the humanities and social sciences employ to study the past and its relationship to the present," and several of the standards emphasize that we must appreciate the value of multiple perspectives. We can offer a quick lesson in cultural point of view by rewriting this summary from a Japanese perspective, starting with the same topic sentence:

> The Japanese bombed the United States in 1941.
> We bombed a place called Pearl Harbor in Hawaii.
> Unfortunately, we didn't completely wipe out the U.S. Navy.
> Fortunately, we had the advantage of surprise.
> Finally, we were at war with the United States.

As any kid who has ever uttered the words *it's not my fault* can attest, there's always more than one side to the story. History offers magnificent chances to teach point of view.

I was recently working with a group of sixth graders from Chardon Middle School in Ohio, and the kids applied this system to their current unit. First we narrowed the subject matter:

What are you studying in social studies?
South America.

Any place in particular?
Brazil.

What about Brazil?
Well, there's the Amazon.

Here is the summary story we wrote as a group about the Amazon:

> The Amazon is the widest river in the world.
> At some points, you can't see across it.
> Unfortunately, it is filled with piranha.
> Fortunately, it is also filled with many species of plants and bugs.
> Finally, it is a dangerous place teeming with life forms.

And the poem version of this story:

Amazon

> Widest river in the world.
> Can't see across.
> Filled with piranha.
> Plants and bugs.
> Dangerous, teeming with life.

Worthy of a poster, if you ask me. And the best part? It took about five minutes.

◆ This is not a writing assignment to be used only once—let it pop up whenever you want to summarize the current unit of study. Are all the details that the student must remember necessarily incorporated in this pattern? Of course not. But by using this writing exercise as an assessment tool, we can see easily what the student writer *thinks* is the most important part of the unit and do a little corrective steering if necessary. Additionally, if we combine a classroom of observations, we can begin to assemble a more complete picture.

◆ Post the poems around the room as reinforcement of content learning.

◆ Assess the accuracy of the content knowledge and students' ability to sequence and prioritize events.

Read My Landscape!

From the Amazon to the Polar Cap, social studies takes us around the world, if not in ninety days, then certainly in nine-month jaunts over twelve years. National geography standard 17 states: "You can't understand history without understanding geography." The geographic features of the environment, both physical and human, strongly influence historical events. By the same token, "You can't understand geography without understanding history." The geographic characteristics of Earth—its lands and people—can only be understood if we trace their evolution over time. I found a review of the geography standards helpful in interpreting the social studies strands. Specifically, they urge teachers to help students develop a "geographer's eye," because after we become familiar with where a place is located, we can "begin to associate physical and human characteristics with that location."

Ten Thematic Strands in Social Studies

III. People, places, and environments. Provides the opportunity for students to utilize language they will use later to *describe varying landforms such as mountains, plateaus, islands, forests, deserts, and oceans* while learning how to *construct and use mental maps that demonstrate an understanding of relative location, direction, size, and shape by using appropriate resources, data sources, and geographic tools.*

I love that phrase, *geographer's eye*, because it so closely parallels what we scribblers refer to as the *poet's eye*, which is an eye for every detail of the "landscape." The major difference seems to be that geographers have some pretty specific terminology to distinguish a rock from a hard place. Geographer jargon includes a litany of terms that must seem as foreign to the average student as the topography of Crete. Check these out—I collected these words in a couple of minutes:

landscape

topography

toponyms

smelting

evapotranspiration

atmospheric

inhabit

pollution

populate

plateau

plains

platelet

migration

municipalities

indigenous

boreal

tributary

subalpine

The Topography of Me

The landscape of my arm
is populated
by surface creases
and forests of hair
extending from subalpine
shoulders
to the flat plateau
of my palm.
My fingers are tributaries
of touch, their
platelets migrate up my streams
to be recycled by my heart
transporting energy
to the atmospheric clouds
inhabiting
the dreams
in my most boreal part.

—SARA HOLBROOK

Great words! They also look like the makings of a vocabulary test, which would be (let's face it) not so fun.

But, they *are* great words. *Maybe* they could be fun. So, I made up a poem (see sidebar) incorporating some of these terms in reference to the landscape of my arm. Not only is this a geography vocabulary lesson, but it is a lesson in mind mapping and metaphor, useful writing tools for the poet and the geographer.

◆ Brainstorm a list of geographic terms and post them on the board.

◆ Instruct kids to pick an object they use every day and know well and chart its landscape. (I'd make the human body as a whole off limits; otherwise, too many kids will streak toward the hills and valleys of Janet Jackson. Tell them to pick a foot, an arm, the scalp. Everyone will be more comfortable and no one will wind up doing hard time.) These might be fun to work on in pairs or small groups.

◆ Have dictionaries, globes, maps, and other geographic resources handy. The only rule is that the words must be used correctly, no matter how absurd the poem turns out to be. You may want to set a minimum number of words to be used, say five or ten, depending on the students' knowledge and ability (extra points available for geographic overachievers).

◆ Give kids an opportunity to showcase their work and tell them to be prepared to defend how they've used the terms. This could turn into a civics lesson as the rest of the class votes on the veracity of their defense.

◆ Assess students' ability to incorporate geographic terms into a poem in a logical and comprehensible way.

The Thing Is

When you were pulling that all-nighter finishing your analysis of the economic impacts of an industrialized society on the common man, did you ever dream that the typewriter you were

Ten Thematic Strands in Social Studies

II. Time, continuity, and change. Encourages students to *identify and use various sources for reconstructing and reinterpreting the past, such as documents, letters, diaries, maps, textbooks, photos,* and others.

VIII. Science, technology, and society. Causes students to *identify and describe examples in which science and technology have changed the lives of people, such as in homemaking, childcare, work, transportation, and communication, as they examine and describe the influence of culture on scientific and technological choices and advancement, such as in transportation, medicine, and warfare;* and gives students an opportunity to *describe examples in which values, beliefs, and attitudes have been influenced by new scientific and technological knowledge.*

IX. Global connections. Invites students to *examine, describe, and analyze the effects of changing technologies.*

working on would so soon become a museum piece? I find myself pausing to explain historical items in some of the poems I wrote not that many years ago. (*You know what albums are, right? Those giant CDs?*)

If you are a fairly recent graduate, maybe you aren't as aware of the short shelf life of the people, events, and gadgets of your youth. Try this on. I was standing at a book table with some teachers last summer and one picked up a biography and slapped it back down again in disgust. "I wish people would stop trying to sell me biographies of Michael Jordan. My kids don't even know who Michael Jordan is." Not only was that a lesson on the half-life of fame, but the teacher's underlying message was, *if the kids don't know who Michael Jordan is, they don't give a dribble about him.*

So how do we engage the MTV generation? One way is through gadgets. Kids love gadgets. As we move from our personal histories to the immediate past, something as simple as an old baseball card or an old campaign button can be a link to understanding the dynamic nature of our culture. Kids will look at their old school pictures and laugh at their hair styles or the outfits they were wearing (amusingly, with no concept that today's outfit will look just as out-of-date in a couple of years). Change is not only the norm for them, it is almost a religion. As a culture, we worship anything new and improved. Yet, in the back of every closet or dresser drawer is some keepsake that speaks to us from another era. A china doll. A broken locket. A pair of wire-rimmed glasses. A vase from the old country.

Street Window

The pawn-shop man knows hunger,
And how far hunger has eaten the heart
Of one who comes with an old keepsake.
Here are wedding rings and baby bracelets,
Scarf pins and shoe buckles, jeweled garters,
Old-fashioned knives with inlaid handles,
Watches of old gold and silver,
Old coins worn with finger-marks.
They tell stories.

—CARL SANDBURG

A Solitary Brush

Oh, mercy.
I do so apologize for my appearance.
It wasn't always like this for me.
You know, I never needed dusting when
I sat on the bureau of my lady.
Those are her initials on my back.
I groomed her hair before an oval mirror
    100 strokes
each night. Every morning I lifted her heavy
    mane into
four tortoiseshell combs. Those were the
    days before
bobbed hair, to be sure. I did my job by
    gaslight
until electricity came in. Rather bright
if you ask me. I was born by candlelight,
woven from the hair of a Persian camel
and tied by the small hands of a
brown-skinned girl
who placed me gently into a box
to be shipped to a shop in New York City
where my lady's hands first touched me.
My lady and the brown-skinned girl are gone
now. I'm all that remains.
A solitary brush.

—SARA HOLBROOK

Ever since high school I've been waiting for someone to ask me who invented the linotype machine so that I can proudly answer, "Otto Merganthaler." (I memorized that for a test in tenth grade and it's been taking up brain space ever since.) That kind of impersonal historical data just doesn't come up that often in real conversation. But there are keepsakes around my house—the clock from my great grandfather's barber shop, a noisemaker from McKinley's inauguration, old family photos—that I find myself showing to friends from time to time, telling the stories behind them, making real connections to the past.

The Carl Sandburg poem, "Street Window," talks about such connections. It is basically a list poem. As he says, the keepsakes of our lives tell stories. And, I humbly add, they can tell poems such as "A Solitary Brush." In fact, they are perfect inspiration for poems because specific objects are—well—specific.

This exercise could involve a field trip to a local pawnshop, thrift store, or museum. While it is engaging to work from family keepsakes (see next exercise), we can broaden our sense of the culture of former generations by visiting other people's things. It is also somewhat less threatening to middle readers, who may be embarrassed by things at home or not have access to anything older than last night's fast-food wrappers, to start with someone else's objects.

◆ Have students chose an object that was once important to someone and has since been discarded.

◆ Have them make up a story about the object from the object's point of view. (My poem "A Solitary Brush" is a model.)

◆ Have students reduce the story to a poem. A snapshot.

◆ Share by posting the poems or finding illustrations for them on the Internet and creating a book of poetry.

◆ Assess students' ability to focus on one object and be able to tie that object to its point in time, reflecting on the culture of a former era.

Family Keepsakes

Family keepsakes are a wonderful source of inspiration for poets and historians alike. Part of our charge, according to the national history standards, is to "initiate historical thinking." What better way than through our family's stuff? Where did this come from? When was it used? Why is it still in the family? What was it used for? All these are questions that can lead students to find a poem in a keepsake and pique their interest in bygone days. Since a family object is likely to have a story behind it, I am providing a poem, "The Shoes" by John Mole, that you can use as a model to help kids keep their ideas focused. Or you can just turn them loose to compose their own poems.

- ◆ Share "The Shoes" with students. Note the pattern of the poem. The first stanza tells us what the shoes were used for, the second stanza tells us what they were *not* used for. Additionally, the first two lines of each stanza are repeated just before the final lines of the stanza. (John Mole is a poet currently working in schools in England, where *Mum* is commonly used instead of *Mom*.)

- ◆ Have students bring in a personal keepsake from home to be the focus of their poems. If the keepsake is valuable or illegal to bring to school (a pocketknife that belonged to Granddad for instance), a photo or hand-drawn picture of the object will do. It's important to identify the approximate year when the item was in use.

- ◆ Have students fold a piece of paper in half lengthwise. On one side, have them list what the object is, its significance to the owner, how it was used. On the other side, have them list what it is not, how it was not used.

- ◆ Have students (individually rather than in pairs or groups) compose their own poems. They can follow the model poem's format or establish their own pattern.

◆ Share the poems aloud or post them in the classroom.

◆ Assess students' ability to focus on one object using the correct vocabulary to indicate time and place and their appreciation of its uniqueness.

Discussing the importance of what we value as people and families and comparing our personal keepsake poems is an ideal way to introduce a section on the importance of respecting diversity and maintaining individuality in a democratic society.

Where Do I Fit In?

We all came from someone and somewhere. Some of us are born into family units and others gravitate toward them. I'm including "Some Families" (see page 148) not as a writing model but as a poem you can share with students to spark a discussion on the nature of family, recognizing that for some kids "family's where they find it." This is important to acknowledge. For this exercise, students work with data collected from the support people in their lives, blood relatives or not.

You want to know a secret? I used to think of my family legacy as a liability. I thought that someone's parents had to have gone to Harvard for that person to declare herself a writer. I didn't realize that just regular folks can pursue this craft. I've learned over the years that I am not alone in this false assumption.

I wrote "Labels" about my personal history, which is a blend of the histories of those who preceded me—from cavemen to my parents. My father was a radiator salesman, my mother loved to dance, my grandmother was a famous-on-our-block cook, and my grandpappy Willie worked on an assembly line building tires for over forty years. Uncle Robert was a mailman, Great Grandfather and Uncle Frank were barbers. All those people contributed to who I am as a citizen of the world and as a writer. Which is why in a democratic society everyone's voice and perspective is important; no two of us have the same heritage.

This is a fun exercise for the beginning of the school year.

♦ Share the poem "Labels" with students. It might be good to make an overhead of this one so that they can look to it for reminders as they build their own family recipe poems. Or give them each a copy.

♦ Have students divide a piece of paper in half lengthwise. On the first half of the paper, have them make a list of significant people in their lives. On the other half, have them list what these people were best known for. Besides being a barber, Uncle Frank was best known for drinking beer and carousing. I left that part out. The major thing he contributed to my education was teaching me how to peel the labels off beer bottles with a straight razor. I left that part out too: This poem has a G rating. Some students will have similar family members. The important thing is to identify what contribution significant people have made in their lives, not just to say, "Uncle Frank was a nutcase."

♦ Have students assemble their information into a poem about the "labels" that make them who they are.

♦ For fun, have students illustrate the poems with family photos. They might even prepare a PowerPoint presentation to share with the class.

♦ Assess students' understanding that we all have unique origins, and that our cultural and family heritage impacts who we are as individuals.

Through the Eye of the Beholder: First-Person Narrative Poems

No news to you, but that portrait of Columbus in your history textbook, painted two hundred years after his death and a couple hundred before the invention of the passport photo, isn't all

Ten Thematic Strands in Social Studies

I. Culture. Gives students an opportunity to *give examples, describe and articulate the implications of cultural diversity, as well as cohesion within and across groups.*

IV. Individual development and identity. Affords students the opportunity to *describe the unique features of one's nuclear and extended families and the way family, gender, ethnicity, nationality, and institutional affiliations contribute to personal identity.*

Labels

People get tagged with these labels,
like African American,
Native American,
White,
Asian, Hispanic,
or Euro-Caucasian—
I just ask that you get my name right.
I'm part Willie,
part Ethel,
part Suzi and Scott.
Part assembly-line worker,
part barber, a lot of dancer
and salesman. Part grocer and mailman.
Part rural, part city, part cook
and part caveman.
I'm a chunk-style vegetable soup
of cultural little bits,
my recipe's unique
and no one label fits.
Grouping folks together
is an individual waste.
You can't know me by just a look,
you have to take a taste.

—SARA HOLBROOK,
Am I Naturally This Crazy?

Some Families

Some families are extended
with grandmothers and aunts,
with cousins by the dozens.
No one has a chance
to say which ones they choose
and which they want removed.
'Cause family's what they got,
a little or a lot.
Some families start small
counting fingers while they grow,
others simply shrink
or take off for the coast.
Some families get divided
and then get rearranged.
When grown-ups choose new partners,
the family dance gets strange.
Some people think the family thing
is mostly overrated.
Some people feel left out,
and some stay isolated.
Some people pick each other
and who knows who's behind it;
they bunch up like bouquets,
and family's where they find it.

—SARA HOLBROOK,
Am I Naturally This Crazy?

that engaging to kids. And let's face it, somebody just made it up. Teachers know that a little prior knowledge goes a long way toward sparking interest and improving comprehension. I expect this is why all those made-up pictures are in the texts in the first place—to make us feel as if we know the guy so that we will want to learn more about him.

As an image-maker myself, I respectfully (and somewhat ruefully) say, nice try. Instead, how about piquing students' interest with a poem? There are plenty of them out there, poems on everything from the practice of Chinese foot binding and the Irish potato famine to labor unions and the Sierra Madres. Poems in the real voices of real people bringing their real experiences to us across continents and ages. Poems from different points of view on the same subject, written at the same time. Such poems provide contemporaneous accounts of world history.

Are these poems all true? Nope. No more than that drawing of Columbus or the one of the first Thanksgiving. *But isn't it the job of the language arts department to teach these poems?* Not a chance. *Why?* Mostly these poems are not considered "good" literature. *Then why bring them into the classroom at all?* Because, even though poetry is not listed in the social studies standards by name (I take issue with this, by the way), artistic creations, folktales, diaries, and literature are.

Historical poems are part of that vast arena known as *original source documents*. Not only that, thanks to modern technology, many of these poems are easily accessible. Students can find them in the library or on the Internet, share them with one another, compare them to the facts in the text, and respond to them in their own words.

One standard we have to keep hammering at constantly in social studies is the necessity of good research. Researching poems written by contemporaneous witnesses to history is a good beginning lesson in finding original source documents that connect students to a time period in a very personal way.

Unfortunately, most school libraries have a very limited supply of personal history poems. They come from raggedy books that have been weeded from the shelves long ago and replaced by fun stuff by Shel Silverstein, Jack Prelutsky, and (oh no) Sara Holbrook, among many others. But it is important for students to know that poets have spoken for the underdog and against injustice across the entire span of history.

Poets have been at the forefront of countless revolutions. Read the biography of almost any poet from almost any culture or time period and you will find that the writer not only came into conflict with institutions and government but also did hard time for expressing opinions through verse. (That doesn't happen in this country as often, which is either a poor reflection on the self-centered nature of our poets or a testament to our First Amendment, probably a combination of both.) Through the voices of the past we learn that police brutality wasn't invented yesterday and that being deprived isn't having just one family car. We learn empathy for people who are not like us when we hear their voices tell their own stories.

While first-person poems may not be easily found in your library, many are now available on the Internet. Not only that, many are way past copyright restrictions, so you can copy them for use in class! I typed "coal mines & children" into my browser and it took me exactly four minutes of research to come up with the following poem about child labor in England by Elizabeth Barrett Browning.

> "For, oh," say the children, "we are weary,
> And we cannot run or leap—
> If we cared for any meadows, it were merely
> To drop down in them and sleep.
> Our knees tremble sorely in the stooping—
> We fall upon our faces, trying to go;
> And underneath our heavy eyelids drooping,
> The reddest flower would look as white as snow.
> For, all day long, we drag our burden tiring,
> Through the coal-dark underground;
> Or, all day we drive the wheels of iron
> In the factories, round and round."
> —Elizabeth Barrett Browning

Here's another from the United States.

The Golf Links Lie So Near the Mill

> The golf links lie so near the mill
> That almost every day
> The laboring children can look out
> And see the men at play.
> —Sarah Cleghorn

I also came across a list of dates and facts regarding child labor. This Act and that Act passed in this year and that.

Which is a more enticing introduction to a unit on the industrial revolution: a list of facts or the poems? Don't we have time to dig up dusty poems? Turn it into a research assignment.

◆ Have students research personal narrative poems related to the topic you are studying. Some examples might be:

Narrower	Wider
The Civil War	War
The California Gold Rush	Prospecting
The Industrial Revolution	Child Labor
Slavery in the United States	Slavery
The Holocaust	Ethnic Cleansing

Narrower topics concentrate on particular periods. Wider topics allow students to compare and contrast people's beliefs and feelings about an issue across cultures and centuries.

◆ Have students copy the poems or print them off the Internet. They can work independently or in pairs.

◆ Have students share the poems with the class, thereby broadening the learning. (Poetry is an aural tradition. When looking for a way for students to share poems with one another, why not put it to a vote? Shall we post the poems on the wall for perusing? Read them aloud? Share them in small groups? Let the class decide and make this a lesson in democracy.)

◆ If poems contain archaic language, ask students to explain the terms and to be able to support their explanations.

◆ Assess students' ability to research and find a poem on the assigned topic and to share the poem with and interpret it for others.

Point of View: A Child's Lament

If I have my own point of view, it follows that everyone else has one too. Sometimes it is the point of view of a person who is blissfully into Grecian urns or trees; sometimes it is the point of

---

Ten Thematic Strands in Social Studies

II. Time, continuity, and change. Helps students develop critical sensitivities, such as empathy and skepticism, regarding altitudes, values, and behavior of people in different historical contexts.

IX. Global connections. Invites students to investigate and demonstrate an understanding of concerns, standards, issues, and conflicts related to universal human rights such as the treatment of children, religious groups, and effects of war.

X. Civic ideals and practices. Causes students to locate, access, analyze, organize, and apply information about selected public issues—recognizing and explaining multiple points of view.

view of a person who has been terribly wronged. The latter voices are heard in a poetic form called a *lament*. Reading others' laments and writing their own will go a long way toward connecting students to the past and letting them sample the brew we call *empathy*, which like coffee is an acquired taste.

In this country, we hold individual rights in high esteem, but such is not and has not been the case everywhere and for all time. Scroll back to the year 110 BC, when a Chinese princess, a child named Hsi-Chun, was sent, for political reasons, to be the wife of a central Asian nomad—K'un Mo, king of the Wu-sun. When she got there, she found her husband old and decrepit. He only saw her once or twice a year, when they drank a cup of wine together. They could not converse, as they had no language in common. A poet named Li Ling wrote a lament for Hsi-Chun.

Lament of Hsi-Chun

My people have married me
In a far corner of Earth:
Sent me away to a strange land,
To the king of the Wu-sun.
A tent is my house,
Of felt are my walls;
Raw flesh my food,
with mare's milk to drink.
Always thinking of my own country,
My heart sad within.
Would I were a yellow stork
And could fly to my old home!
    —Li Ling in *170 Chinese Poems,*
      translated by Arthur Waley.
London: Alfred A. Knopf, 1919, p. 75

A poem like this naturally leads to a barrage of questions about arranged marriages, child brides, and the rights of women and young people. Although the construction of this lament is somewhat archaic, the words are easily understood. Students can identify with Hsi-Chun's powerlessness because, like her, they are children. Kids also identify with Hsi-Chun's sense of isolation.

Throughout history there are countless incidents where because of migration, impending danger, or economic hardships, children have been sent away from their parents. You can use this little poem as a pattern for kids to write their own laments, from a single point of view that parallels the subject you are studying.

◆ Share the "Lament of Hsi-Chun" with students. Discuss the point of view and her plight. We don't know her age exactly, but custom would indicate Hsi-Chun was no more than twelve or thirteen.

◆ Build a bridge between Hsi-Chun's plight and a child's plight related to your unit of study.

◆ Have students write a lament from the perspective of a child in the appropriate period.

◆ Remind them to be sure to keep the historical facts consistent. Here are a few examples of how this could be done, depending on what they're studying:

> My people have sent me *to work in this factory or mine.*
> My people have sent me *to this Indian school.*
> My people have sent me *to a new land.*
> My people have sent me *to fight in this war.*

◆ Share the poems aloud as a class or in small groups. Students should be prepared to defend their points of view as the aggrieved parties.

◆ Assess students' ability to write from one point of view and the accuracy of the historical data they present.

And Justice for All: Poets Reflect on Current Events

The standards threw me a bit of a curve when I went looking for one related to human rights violations in the United States, visions of Joe McCarthy, General Custer, slavery, and a few other constitutional incongruities dancing in my head. According to

Ten Thematic Strands in Social Studies

X. Civic ideals and practices. Helps students to identify *key ideals of the United States' democratic republican form of government, such as individual human dignity, liberty, justice, equality, and the rule of law;* and to *discuss their application in specific situations* in addition to *actions citizens can take to influence public policy decisions.* Helps students recognize *how the "common good" can be strengthened through strategies that consider a range of options for citizen action.* Causes students to *demonstrate understanding of concerns, standards, issues, and conflicts related to universal human rights.*

the standards, human rights violations only exist in the global connections strand. I realize these standards are written broadly and are not to be confused with actual curriculum content (World War II isn't mentioned either, and it was kind of an event). Still, I had to search for a standard to which to attach the concept of people speaking out against injustice in this country; one might assume it didn't exist.

So I propose a new standard in strand 7—production, distribution, and consumption (the strand that deals with economics). It would read: *identify examples of how selfish, ignorant, greedy people sometimes take control of a democratic government for their own gain and in turn abuse society and groups of people.*

Now that I have that off my chest, I did find one little mention in the civics ideals and practices strand that implies that

---

One day I was visiting John Greenleaf Whittier Elementary School in Royal Oak, Michigan. The first assembly was for primary kids, so when I asked them if they knew who Whittier was and they had no idea, I wasn't too bothered. When I asked the intermediate kids and none knew, I was a bit more concerned. When I looked to the teachers sitting on the periphery of the assembled students and they shook their heads too, I had to do a little commercial for the ol' coot.

"You all have to learn who this dude was!" I said, "He was very cool. He's not just another dead white guy. He was an abolitionist, wrote poems exposing the truth about slavery, and went around screaming his poems in people's faces on street corners and at town halls."

There was a meager stirring of interest, but unfortunately I didn't have the poems at hand. Too bad. Whittier wrote some pretty stirring stuff. English majors *may* remember Whittier for his domesticated nature poem "Snowbound." Somehow his more rabid political poems have been homogenized out of our textbooks, probably on the excuse that they are not considered "good poetry."

Of course Longfellow isn't that respected as a poet either, but we've all been assigned "The Midnight Ride of Paul Revere." I expect there are reasons that this is so—that some historical poems have been slighted over the years—but I don't want to get into that. Just know that there are volumes of poetry on subjects related to slavery, the Civil War, and abolition from all different perspectives.

These curiosities are notes from our ancestors written on the backs of envelopes, shared around hearths, and screamed from the rooftops. They are worth remembering even if—especially if—they have been rejected by the English literature types. Consider them folk art, made by and for common folk.

---

sometimes our country's actions may not reflect our ideals. I guess that's where we can skinny in a mention of slavery. And I found extensive language to indicate that folks can take "citizen action" when they don't agree with policy. Enter the poets.

John Greenleaf Whittier (see sidebar) is just one of any number of poets who over the years have used their poetic voice to attempt to influence public opinion, a tradition that continues today. When President George W. Bush was setting in place a plan to invade Iraq, the first lady promptly canceled a White House gathering of poets, who were scheduled to celebrate the works of Walt Whitman and Emily Dickinson, because staffers were worried the event would become political. That Laura Bush ever thought she could convene a symposium of poets to speak about Whitman and have it not be centered on politics and peace only points to the importance of reading a poet's entire works, not just the cute ditties often chosen for textbooks. Superfluous as poets may appear to be in a bottom-line world, they are still considered dangerous. You just never know what one will say—or do; like rent a hall to spout off against slavery. That was Whittier's forum of choice. But he was not opposed to street corners either.

As you enter a unit on any period of time or area of the world, I would urge you to ask students a question leading them to some research: *What were the poets saying?* Poets are often on the leading edge of change. They are the canaries that warn us of danger in societies' coal mines.

♦ Share a poem about injustice, such as "The Farewell" or "The Slave Ship," with students (fragments of the complete poems, whittled down to fit a standard class period are fine). When

The Farewell

Gone, gone—sold and gone,
To the rice-swamp dank and lone.
Where the slave-whip ceaseless swings,
Where the noisome insect stings,
Where the fever demon strews
Poison with the falling dews,
Where the sickly sunbeams glare
Through the hot and misty air—
Gone, gone—sold and gone,
To the rice-swamp dank and lone.
From Virginia's hills and waters—
Woe is me, my stolen daughters!

Gone, gone—sold and gone,
To the rice-swamp dank and lone.
There no mother's eye is near them,
There no mother's ear can hear them;
Never, when the torturing lash
Seams their back with many a gash,
Shall a mother's kindness bless them,
Or a mother's arms caress them.
Gone, gone—sold and gone,
To the rice-swamp dank and lone.
From Virginia's hills and waters—
Woe is me, my stolen daughters!

—JOHN GREENLEAF WHITTIER (1838)

the language is archaic, I like to divide the class into small groups and give each group a verse to decipher.

◆ Explain that the poem (and others like it) can be labeled a "reader response" to a current event.

◆ Discuss how actions like this can influence public policy.

◆ Have small groups of students find an example of a similar poem; there is a wealth of poetry out there from which to choose.

◆ Many poems were written for a public forum, so have the kids act them out. They may choose to perform only a portion of the poem, but they will find it hard to cut out any dramatic details.

◆ Perhaps extend the lesson by asking students to respond to a current event with a factual poem constructed with the express purpose of changing public opinion. (Have them choose a news article, make a list of details it brought out, and turn that list into a poem. Or see the next section, "It's Not Fair.")

◆ Assess students' participation in the discussion. If writing a poem is included, assess the accuracy of its data.

The Slave Ship*

"All ready?" cried the captain;
    "Ay, ay!" the seamen said;
"Heave up the worthless lubbers—
    the dying and the dead."
Up from the slave-ship's prison
    Fierce, bearded heads were thrust—
"Now let the sharks look to it—
    Toss up the dead ones first!"

Corpse after corpse came up—
    Death had been busy there;
Where every blow is mercy,
    Why should the Spoiler spare?
Corpse after corpse they cast
    Sullenly from the ship,
Yet bloody with the traces
    Of fetter-link and whip.

Gloomily stood the captain,
    With his arms upon his breast,
With his cold brow sternly knotted,
    And his iron lip compress'd.
"Are all the dead dogs over?"
    Growled through that matted lip—
"The blind ones are no better,
    Let's lighten the good ship."

Hark! From the ship's dark bosom,
    The very sounds of Hell!
The ringing clank of iron—
    The maniac's short, sharp yell!—
The hoarse, low curse, throat stifled—
    The starving infant's moan—
The horror of a breaking heart
    Pour'd through a mother's groan!

Up from the loathsome prison
    The stricken blind ones came:
Below, had all been darkness—
    Above, was still the same.
Yet the holy breath of Heaven
    Was sweetly breathing there,
And the heated brow of fever
    Cool'd in the soft sea air.

"Overboard with them, shipmates!"
    Cutlass and dirk were plied;
Fettered and blind, one after one,
    Plunged down the vessel's side.
The sabre smote above—
    Beneath, the lean shark lay,
Waiting with wide and bloody jaw
    His quick and human prey. . . .

—JOHN GREENLEAF WHITTIER (1834)

*The French ship Le Rodeur, with a crew of twenty-two men and with one hundred and sixty negro slaves sailed from Bonny, in Africa, April 1819. On approaching the line, a terrible malady broke out—an obstinate disease of the eyes—contagious, and altogether beyond the resources of medicine. It was aggravated by the scarcity of water among the slaves (only half a wine glass per day being allowed to an individual), and by the extreme impurity of the air in which they breathed. By advice of the physician, they were brought upon deck occasionally; but some of the poor wretches, locking themselves in each other's arms leaped overboard, in the hope, which so universally prevails among them, of being swiftly transported to their own homes in Africa. To check this, the captain ordered several, who were stopped in the attempt, to be shot, or hanged, before their companions. The disease extended to the crew; and one after another were smitten with it, until only one remained unaffected. Yet even this dreadful condition did not preclude calculation; to save the expense of supporting slaves rendered unsalable, and to obtain grounds for a claim against the underwriters, thirty-six of the negroes, having become blind, were thrown into the sea and drowned.

In the midst of their dreadful fears lest the solitary individual, whose sight remained unaffected, should also be seized with the malady, a sail was discovered. It was the Spanish slaver Leon. The same disease had been there; and horrible to tell, all the crew had become blind. Unable to assist each other, the vessels parted. The Spanish ship has never been heard of. The Rodeur reached Guadaloupe on the 21st of June; the only man who had escaped the disease, and had thus been enabled to steer the slaver into port, caught it three days after his arrival. (Speech of M. Benjamin Constant, in the French Chamber of Deputies, June 17, 1820; quoted in Poems of John G. Whittier, New York: A. L. Burt, 1901, pp. 141–43.)

It's Not Fair!

Kids of all ages have views on what they see as fair and not fair. In fact they are pretty clear about it. It isn't until we start to get some years on us that all that black and white starts to fade into shades of gray. Change that has come about in the world often has happened as a result of some kind of compromise, not all of which is fair to all parties, including other species and the environment. One way to engage kids in current or past events is to have them try to determine what's fair and what's not from different points of view.

It is our right and responsibility as citizens to have opinions on issues beyond the next bug-crunching reality television series and whatever future inanities various media see fit to foist on us. And citizens must be able to express these opinions coherently, logically, and in an informed way. (How's that for soapbox oratory?) In this activity, students are going to let loose with some political opinions. And if you think kids aren't interested in anything beyond the new releases at the video store, they just may surprise you.

I was working with a group of eighth graders at Gompers Secondary School in San Diego the month prior to the beginning of the war in Iraq. I began by passing out index cards to the class and having each student complete this sentence on his or her card: *It's not fair that* . . . Responses looked like a page from the editorial section of the *Los Angeles Times:*

◆ *It's not fair that* women do not get to receive more privileges like men do.

◆ *It's not fair that* men get more attention and better jobs than women do.

◆ *It's not fair that* gas prices went up.

◆ *It's not fair that* people stereotype all teenagers as careless people and smokers.

- *It's not fair that* I always get blamed for something my little sister does because I'm older and my mom says, "You shouldn't let her do that."

- *It's not fair that* people make fun of gays and lesbians.

- *It's not fair that* Osama Bin Laden is still alive.

- *It's not fair that* Michael Jackson is getting picked on.

- *It's not fair that* the war threat is getting bigger.

- *It's not fair that* we have to worry about war.

- *It's not fair that* little kids can't walk home from school without getting attacked.

- *It's not fair that* there are abortions in the world.

How about that for a summary of current events for March of 2003?

- Pass out index cards or scraps of paper and have students complete the sentence, *It's not fair that* _____. To expand their ability to research current events, you may wish to have them use newspapers and magazines to spark ideas.

- Post the cards around the room.

- Have the kids, in pairs, "shop" for a topic of interest to both parties. (This takes a while; it is an initial experiment in compromise.)

- After student pairs have identified a topic, have each pair rip a single sheet of paper in half lengthwise, each taking a half.

- Ask each member of the writing team to choose a point of view from which to write. (Even though they have agreed on the topic, they can still take different points of view.) For instance, if the topic is "It's not fair that gas prices went up," one student could take the point of view of a driver of an

Adrenaline

Made you run.
Made you run.
        Thanks a lot
        adrenaline.
Stop your whining,
I got you there.
        Yeah. Like a panting dog
        with stand-up hair.
You would have arrived
sometime next week.
        You blew my cool.
        You made me freak.
I like to push you
to the max.
        Great.
        Now take a hike
        and I'll relax.

—SARA HOLBROOK,
By Definition

SUV and one could take the point of view of a gas station owner who is tired of getting yelled at. (In the class in San Diego, one pair of girls decided to write about the 2003 impending war in Iraq. One chose the point of view of a mother, the other that of Uncle Sam.)

◆ Have them, working independently, make a list of arguments defending their points of view. It is important for each student to assume the identity of the character chosen, try on his shoes, speak in her voice.

◆ Have two students read a poem for two voices aloud to the class. (See sidebar examples, one for younger kids "Adrenaline" and one for middle schoolers "We Own This Town". Plenty more are available in your library. For a start, look in Paul Fleishman's Newbery award–winning book *Joyful Noise;* there are more in my book *Wham! It's a Poetry Jam.* Political poems for elementary kids are tough to come by, so it's up to them to create their own in class. You could use one of the next student samples.)

I wrote the following poem with a friend of mine, Anthony Rucker, who goes by the stage name of Da Boogie Man. He is twenty years younger than I am, African American, and big enough to play center on a professional football team. To say that we look at the world from different points of view is an understatement. We first performed this poem at the National Poetry Slam in 1995. Fresh from my work experience at the law firm, I had this notion that some of the corporate criminals I had come to know were no more than gang members in seventeen-hundred-dollar suits. So I wrote a short poem about it. Boogie cut the poem up in pieces and interspersed his own stanzas about gangs from a different perspective and gave it back to me. We continued to trade back and forth until we had essentially what you see here (the original, which has a few controversial words in it, is in my *Chicks Up Front* book).

We Own This Town

From downtown to the suburbs,
the streets are mine.
People complain, but they all want me
to do what I do.
Stores get insurance claims,
people have someone to blame,
and cops get to keep their jobs.

So you want to be one of the gang
down at the Union Club.
Boy, you've got to change your . . . colors.
Our colors are gray and . . . white.

I do what I'm forced to do, if I had other options
I'd make other choices.
But now, I choose to survive.

It's survival of the fittest, downtown,
no welfare programs here, it's natural selection.
We are the corporate heads and
out of our hats come the names of
who and what's going to work in this town.
Need a building, a stadium? Done!

If I put a gun to your head
I can take what you own.
If I want power,
I take power. Done!

Not give-and-take, take and give.
We are benevolent,
dictating contributions to the ballet,
good public relations.
Not food banks, son.
Poor write-offs just don't make good press.

Damn the press and Ted Koppel.
I rob from the rich and give
to poor little ol' me.
I even got me a crew,
everybody needs a Board of Trustees.
Nobody can fight the world alone.
You might not respect us even in numbers,
so we carry bullets and chrome.

Together, one for all and all for us.
Power!
We own this town.
Everybody's on our turf.
I can't afford to be softhearted,
it's kill or be killed, no POWs
coming out of this war.
And the money?
It's just a way of keeping score.

Money ain't nothin' to a dead man,
you better check the body count.
We didn't ask for war,
you gave it to us.
So either poop or get off the pot.
I have to be true to the game,
compassion in battle will get a brother shot.

Come on over here and meet the homeboys—
best part, we hardly ever go home.
Hey you, use the back steps.
You look good in the bedroom,
but not in the boardroom,
this way to the ladies' waiting room, miss.

And all you witches can wait
until hell freezes over.
'Cause if your baby dies,
if you die,
if a cop dies
and I don't die?
Everything is fine.
When all competition is gone
the game will be over

and the world will be mine.
In guns we trust.

Our motto is: in tradition we trust.
And speaking of trust,
son, put down that gun.
That's no way to rob a bank.

◆ Discuss the poem. Who do these two voices belong to? What do they have in common? What's different about them?

◆ Ask the student pairs to go back to their lists, to put the paper they divided back together. Ask them to compare and contrast the lists, to see what is the same and what is different given their two different points of view. Maybe they can think of some other points as they look over partners' lists.

◆ Ask the kids to put their poems together then (either blocks of copy or single lines traded back and forth) to create a poem for two voices.

◆ Have the teams take turns presenting the poems for two voices to the rest of the class. (Bring in a soapbox or dairy crate for kids to stand on to recreate an American tradition.)

◆ Assess students' ability to compromise, establish a clear point of view, and present their poems aloud. This is a democratic forum: Did they participate, treat everyone with respect, learn new things?

Here are two poems written by the Gompers students:

It's not fair, my boy could die.
    I need your son to go to war.
I don't know when he's going to be safe.
    But he has to go for his country.
He may never come home to me again.
    But he will die with honor.
Honor or no honor. I don't want him to go.
    He will have to go anyway.
Think twice before sending people to die with "honor."
        —Letycya and Curina, Grade 8

Everyone should have
equal rights.
Stand up and fight
for what you like.
Women are not being
treated like men,
only the Lord can comprehend.

Women should be treated fairly
men are rarely comprehending
that women are really smart.
They put their babies
into Head Start.

—T.T. and Natasha, Grade 8

One difference I noticed working with Katie Lufkin's sixth-grade social studies class is that, at the ripe old age of eleven or twelve, the students seemed to have a much more narrow view of the world than the eighth graders at Gompers. The students were much more focused on family and home life and less tuned into world events. Establishing points of view other than their own was a challenge for Katie's sixth graders. When we finished the exercise, Katie turned to me and said she was going to have to reinforce two writing skills with her students: point of view and how to build an argument using specific facts. She was afraid I would be disappointed with the results of the students' writing, but I found it exciting that our poetry lesson was able to help her in this assessment of her class and students' capabilities: We were working in January, with proficiency tests looming in March.

If your students aren't skilled enough to write poems independently, you can create a poem together as a class. At Gompers, kids in a 7.5 class (kids repeating seventh grade, mostly because of difficulties reading and understanding English as a second language) created the following piece:

         IT'S NOT FAIR
That there is war
         IT'S NOT FAIR
Gangs on the street
         IT'S NOT FAIR
My brother gets what he wants
         IT'S NOT FAIR
That drive-bys kill
         IT'S NOT FAIR
The innocent die
         IT'S NOT FAIR
That we're mistreated
         IT'S NOT FAIR
I'm in 7.5
         IT'S NOT FAIR
I didn't pass to eighth
         IT'S NOT FAIR
That people fight
         IT'S NOT FAIR
Sixteen to drive
         IT'S NOT FAIR
People mistreated 'cuz of their color
         IT'S NOT FAIR
The homeless have no homes
         IT'S NOT FAIR
Police give tickets for throwing trash
         IT'S NOT FAIR
People tag our school
         IT'S NOT FAIR
         IT'S NOT FAIR
Stop the violence
Stop the violence
         IT'S NOT FAIR!

Such an exercise is portable. Imagine moving it to Birmingham, Alabama, in 1963. To the gold rush. To the dust bowl. Take it with you in your classroom time travels.

Standards

II. Time, continuity, and change. Provides students an opportunity to *identify and describe selected historical periods and patterns of change within and across cultures.*

III. People, places, and environments. Helps students *examine, interpret, and analyze physical and cultural patterns and their interactions, such as land use, settlement patterns, cultural transmission of customs and ideas, and ecosystem changes; and describe ways that historical events have been influenced by, and have influenced, physical and human geographic factors in local, regional, national, and global settings.*

That Day Like Any Other

Poet-philosopher Wendell Berry says, "If you don't know where you are, you don't know *who* you are." Being able to place ourselves in other times and places on the planet is key to understanding the people who actually lived there then. What was life like for the average person? How did they do their marketing and take care of their children? What was their relationship to the land and economy?

"None Knew" is a poem that I admire because it draws such a realistic image of a town on a day that seemed ordinary enough, but after that day the world was forever changed. It takes us somewhere we have never been before, walks us up and down the road meeting the townsfolk. The poem can be used as a model for students' first-person poetry accounts of some of the other days that have changed the world.

The day Lincoln was born (or shot).

The day the Declaration of Independence was signed.

The day the twin towers fell.

The day Rosa Parks refused to give up her seat.

The day Mother Theresa was born.

The day Knute Rockne invented the forward pass.

The day Barry Gordy founded Motown Records.

None Knew (April 22, 1870)

A day like any Russian day.
The same grey drabness grimed the street.

A grim voice roared, "Get on your way!"
the policeman at his beat.

The priest, in gaudy vestments, proud
through the cathedral-service sidled;

and drunk from dawn, a rowdy crowd
around the dramshop entry idled.

The marketwomen bawled with passion,
buzzing like flies on honeypots.

Middle-class wives, all mad for fashion,
poked through the stalls of cotton-lots.

At an official door, dismayed
and awed, a peasant dumbly pored

over the faded prints displayed,
the yellowing orders on the board.

The fireman in the tower went round,
and round again, like a chained bear.

The sergeant rattled oaths and frowned
on soldiers drilling in the square.

The carts went winding to the quays
where flour-white dockers took the load.

A student, ragged at the knees,
among the guards, went down the road.

A worker—boozy wits astray—
was bawling someone out, exploding:
"Goodbye poor student all forlorn. . . ."

None knew. Beneath her cross of scorn
our Russia stumbled on her way.

That day like any other day,
that day of days—Lenin was born.

—Demyan Byedny, April 22, 1927

(From Russian Poetry 1917–1955, selected and translated by Jack
Lindsay, pp. 48–49. London and Southhampton: The Camelot Press,
for John Lane The Bodley Head, 1957.)

Some days are significant because of life or death issues, some
because of their cultural impact. To write poems like this the

writer needs explicit knowledge of the period, place, and time. Such an assignment may be a recurring one in different units.

- Share the poem "None Knew (April 22, 1870)" with students.

- Because the poem has some difficult words in it, it is more easily digestible in small pieces. To that end, I've added lines between the chunks of thought. Duplicate the poem, cut it up into sections, and distribute the sections to pairs of students.

- Have students figure out the section. They may have to do some research in the dictionary, but if every pair only has a sentence, this isn't an insurmountable task.

- Have the pairs present their sections and explain what is happening so that the class can appreciate the rich, visual detail in the poem.

- Ask students, working in pairs or individually, to capture a day related to a topic you are studying. Have them list details of what might have been happening on the street and then use those details to create a poem.

- Ask kids to illustrate, display, or perform their poems for the class.

- Assess students' ability to decipher their sections of the model poem and to build their own poem out of old bones.

Ever play "look" at a cafeteria table? Take a bite of the mystery meat, mash it around in your mouth, open wide, and yell, "Look!" Okay, you never did, but your friends did. I know.

Well, a good poem is like that. The poet takes a bite out of life, chews a bit, and then opens wide. Whether we are studying poems resurrected from the dust of the past or creating our own, the images will stay with students long past test time, giving them lasting lessons in culture, history, diversity, respect for others, and finally in the value of recording events as they come along as a means of finding our place in the world.

Epilogue: Always Have an Agenda

Here was my agenda: I would go to a bed-and-breakfast in the country for one week to get in touch with nature, write a novel and seventeen poems, catch up on sleep, relax, and lose ten pounds. I'd been racing through short nights and airports all spring. Creativity requires leisure time. I sure wasn't going to find it on carousel 8 in the baggage claim area—I needed to get out of town to someplace quiet and focus. I'd been up to my ears in static for months. It was time to sit down and tune in. Every day, I would write from sunup till 7 PM, strap on my sneakers, break for a walk, come home and edit, and live on fruit and carrot sticks. It was a plan.

Emily, the resident dog, a slight brown streak, elected to join me on my walk the first evening without a vote. She just came loping alongside, tongue lapping a little to the left. This was an up-and-down-hills, no-nonsense, I-have-to-loose-weight kind of walk. Three miles out, about-face, clip-clip, three miles back to the farm, no resting on the sneakers. Past some corn, a few trailers, and a man in a lawn chair with a sign tacked to his fence reading *Here lives one old lady and one old fart*. The old fart smiled and hallooed as I passed the second time. Twice past made us neighbors.

Over another hill and old Emily took off into the tall grasses to the left in a field that stretched golden green, here and there flowers, the wide sunlit expanse interrupted by only one tumble-down barn. Emily leapt like a gazelle through the tall grasses, up-disappear, up-disappear, cross-stitching some pattern only in her head until I couldn't see her anymore.

I whistled and called; she was nowhere. Now, this was a country dog who had never seen a leash, and we were in her backyard, be it ever so huge. Still, I was nervous to leave her a mile from home, so I stopped, tapped my foot, and whistled again. I had two legs and she had four, which clearly marked me the responsible party.

"Emileeee." No dog.

First came the mother rabbit across the road. She stopped, sized me up quickly as no threat in *those* shoes, and disappeared into the bush. Came one of the babies. Came another. Another. No Emily. I walked in circles, my heart rate slowing, my impatience accelerating. Clearly, Emily had her own agenda when it came to rabbits.

She appeared. But immediately back into the grass with a leap of enthusiasm.

"Emily!" I tried logic. "The rabbits crossed the road."

But she had followed me down to where the road dead-ended without any explanation on my part, so she naturally didn't offer one to me as she pursued the departed rabbits, popping heads-up to disappear again.

I tried name-calling. "Come on, you dummy."

I tried threats. "Next time you stay home, girl." Just my luck. I come here to escape responsibility and the helter-skelter of the day-to-day, I need to stay on task, and here I stand, waiting on a nowhere dog that guilt won't let me leave behind.

"I have work to do, dog. Let's move it." *Mumble, mumble.* I could hear my laptop computer humming quietly back at the house, its cursor pulsing and internal clock tracking time. My leisure time, which was limited and ticking away.

"Emileeee." Nothing. What seemed to me impertinent, no doubt to her very natural and pertinent—civil disobedience revisited. I came here to write and get back to nature, not track down a Thoreauvian dog.

A flash of red in a bush fifty yards off. Another. And on the wire overhead and then to the treetops, at least five or six cardinals tacking against the wind and calling back and forth.

I tried trickery. Ran up and down the hill a couple times, "Come on, girl, come on," hoping she would catch the spirit and race me to the top of the hill. No fool, that Emily. The trick had no effect on her. On me? It made me sweat.

I leaned against a fence lifting my hair to the scant breeze. Which way was west? I turned around, finding the setting sun to my right; the winding roads had left me without my instinctive compass. Pocketing my hands for a rest, I noticed that the post supporting the wire fence was just an old branch, weatherworn how many years, gathered one day for this purpose. A branch. Not unlike the branches at home that I routinely break into the prescribed less-than-three-foot length and put out on the tree lawn. This one put to use here where sticks have life after death and no one has a tree lawn.

The tall grass had a virtual pond of flowering purple clover in its midst. What had appeared to be still, now quite vacant of rabbits, turned out to be alive with bees. Chubby bees in downy black-and-yellow coats, working against the clock. Punching their flowers and humming noisily as they worked.

My heart rate now well below weight-loss velocity, I gave up and sat down in the gravel. The road was still warm from the sun's friction and felt like a heating pad against my thighs as I stretched out my legs. The clouds looked like soap breaking up after a bath and the sky was slate to the north. *Perhaps the rain the fields are needing.* I watched as the light turned from white to golden to green. The sunset wasn't happening up over the hill but all around me. Its coolness grabbed me by the arms, but I still had the warmest seat in the house. I plotted tomorrow's walk and wondered why a tumbled barn on the horizon had no house overlooking its demise. Close by birds, far off dogs, humming bees. No answer, just nature working toward the end of day reclaiming the land once taken to crops and a barn. It took half an hour for the sun to set.

When out of the grass, a bounder. Emily. Brown ears flopping, tail wagging ruffles, she hopped up over me to the top of the hill. And a bark, direct. No tricks.

"Come on, girl," she panted, and smiled broadly from the middle of the road, showing me the way. She summed up her opinion of me in one last bark over her shoulder as she took off toward home. "You dummy."